the LITTLE CHURCH
that COULD
raising SMALL church esteem

STEVEN E. BURT AND HAZEL ANN ROPER

Judson Press
Valley Forge

Library of Congress Cataloging-in-Publication Data

Burt, Steven E., 1949-
    [Raising small church esteem]
    The little church that could : raising small church esteem / Steven E. Burt, Hazel Ann Roper.
        p. cm.
    Previously published: Raising small church esteem. [Bethesda, MD]: The Alban Institute, 1992.
    Includes bibliographical references.
    ISBN 0-8170-1370-9 (pbk. : alk. paper)
    1. Small churches. 2. Pastoral theology. I. Roper, Hazel Ann. II. Title.

BV637.8.B88 2001
    254—dc21   00-055468

Printed in the U.S.A.
06 05 04 03 02 01 00
10 9 8 7 6 5 4 3 2 1

CONTENTS

INTRODUCTION

At a doctoral class on theological reflection, we asked our colleagues to engage in word association beginning with the word *small*. When a large number of negative combinations emerged, we turned to *Roget's Thesaurus* for synonyms. The group's responses paralleled the proportion of negatively charged words listed in the thesaurus! *Roget's* offered: scarcity, insignificance, minimum, trifle, scrap, shred, tag, rag, handful, drop in the bucket, stunted, sawed off, tiny, puny, wee, runty, miniature, scanty, limited, lesser, meager, few, sparse, slight, inappreciable, inconsiderable, mere, unimportant, trivial, and inconsequential. If *small* carries this negative connotation, what happens when *small* is linked to "church" to make "small church"?

Is the small church perceived to be one or all of the above synonyms? That makes one huge strike against us. If society's attitudes reflect the belief that small is negative, how will that affect the esteem of the small church? If there is truth in the concept of self-fulfilling prophecies and to the theory that we live up to others' expectations of us—"You've never been any good"—what does that mean for the small church and its ministries?

When we use the word-association technique in workshops with small congregations, the phrase "small church" invariably produces the following responses: limited human resources, faithful remnant, handful, too few doing too much, dependence on denomination, petty bickering, lack of privacy, money worries, inexperienced and entry-level clergy, limited programs, physical plant millstones, building upkeep difficulties, clergy turnover, and many more. It becomes clear very quickly that these folks are keenly aware of the "negative" side of the small church.

The participants, however, also provide us with a balance of positive phrases: close-knit, community, family, friendly, caring, intimacy, fulfilling, participatory, skill developing, trusting, cooperative, mutual support, valuing. The leaders recognize the struggles and shortcomings of the small church. Yet these people experience tremendous satisfaction from being part of an institution frequently devalued in a society that heralds "bigger is better."

"Small church" needs a working definition for the purposes of this book. Many have attempted to *numerically* define the small church—number of members, communicants, pledging units, and worshipers averaged per annum. We resist these data for the most part. Figures seem too arbitrary, like describing a person as "a hundred pounds of clay." Numbers are most often used when judging the small church, singling out its inadequacies, or devaluing its effectiveness.

In his pioneering book, *Making the Small Church Effective,* Carl Dudley offers what is perhaps closest to our definition of the small church when he describes it in relational terms as "a single cell of caring."[1] In *Looking in the Mirror,* Lyle Schaller also avoids the trap of the numbers game when he suggests that the line of demarcation between small and medium-sized churches is not numerical but *behavioral.* In an imaginative style, Schaller compares the behaviors of small churches to contrary-minded cats and affectionate collies—both whole, unified entities; middle-sized churches are compared to gardens—multi-celled, compartmentalized, specialized, with different sections for peas, carrots, and turnips.[2] (This interesting notion is treated in chapter three.)

Considering Dudley's and Schaller's concepts together, we can point to something other than a numerically determined definition. After all, a church with eighty people at worship might act middle-sized while another church with 110 at worship might act as a small church—based on their behaviors. Numbers prove to be inaccurate in revealing whether a church is a small church. Based on our experience and understanding, we have chosen to describe the small church *experientially* as a living, caring, changing community.[3]

And what of esteem? We believe it is more than morale, though morale is an important part of esteem. Esteem has to do with identity and well-being; it is connected with the discovery or recovery of one's God-given individuality. Once that identity is valued and claimed, one can be true to it. Esteem sometimes means, with God's help, recreating and reclaiming a new preferable identity.

Organizational psychologist Marsha Sinetar has this to say about the topic: "Self-esteem is just an idea we have about ourselves . . . about our competence, our worth, and our power . . . a picture we have in our minds about ourselves . . . [one] we start making when we are little babies, vulnerable to grownups' ways, deep under the spell of their perceptions of us."[4]

She further suggests that we often lose sight of our identity and self-esteem, or find it distorted, damaged, or hidden. "We begin listening to the opinion (and tone) of everyone important to us . . . [and we learn to] judge ourselves . . . [Self-esteem is] our special private judgment about our special private way of being in the world—our sense about how or whether our uniqueness fits with the rest of the world."[5]

Often small churches, like human beings, lose sight of that self-picture. In its place they develop a poor self-image with its attendant lack of self-esteem. *They accept a self-image dictated by society and the dominant culture, an image thrust on them by peer pressure, an image reinforced by failure or depression.* Small churches allow outside forces and people (some very important to them) to shape them. In the process, their own God-given self-image is distorted, if not buried. The task is to rediscover that healthy self-image and to recover the small church's esteem. If the existing self-portrait is unhealthy, then the task is to transform it and, with God's help and guidance, to find a better one. Sinetar continues: "[Self-esteem is feelings] and self-pictures that we ourselves make real, and only we can change it for the better, for our own good, forever."[6]

Raising esteem is a salvation we believe to be possible not only for individuals, but for corporate entities such as small congregations.

Before we proceed, we need to introduce ourselves as the team responsible for writing this book. It will become apparent that we approach issues from slightly different angles.

The most obvious difference in the individual perceptions, perspectives, and sensitivities is that of gender. The next is affiliation. While both of us are clergy, Hazel is an American Baptist; Steve, formerly a United Methodist minister, now serves the United Church of Christ and the American Baptists. Both of us have pastored small churches and supervised field education students (Hazel having received both the Rural Pastor of the Year Award from her denomination as well as Andover Newton Theological School's Telfer Award for excellence in field education supervision). But our more recent job positions provide us with varying experiences and approaches.

Hazel is a middle judicatory leader, an associate executive/field minister for the American Baptist Churches of New York State. Her job involves facilitating pastor-church matches, engaging in conflict management, and helping congregations clarify their identities. A high percentage of the hundred-plus churches in Hazel's region are small churches. On a daily basis she deals with the issue of esteem in small congregations.

Steve has been a national small-church consultant since 1984, and has directed both the Small Church Program at the Missouri School of Religion (MSR) and the Connecticut Ecumenical Small Church Project. As a consultant he has provided weekend identity assessments or "church checkups" for small churches, and as director of both the Missouri and Connecticut projects, he has trained two-person lay/clergy teams on-site in the assessment process. He is a popular speaker, having keynoted the regional and national small-church events of nearly two dozen denominations, and regularly leads workshops around the country discussing small-church dynamics, leadership, and esteem. In the mid-1980s he organized and trained the Vermont/New Hampshire Ecumenical Lay Preaching Group, whose fifteen lay speakers provided pulpit supply to dozens of area churches. He has taught courses on small churches in the joint MSR/Eden Seminary Master of Theological Studies Program and in MSR's lay pastor certificate program. At MSR he was also the founding editor of *The Small Church Newsletter.* One of his books, *Activating Leadership in the Small Church,* published in 1988 as the lead-off hitter in Judson Press's "Small Church in Action Series," is in its third printing and is a staple on many seminaries' practice-of-ministry reading lists. Most of his ministry time lately has gone into interim pastor work with small churches in transition.

Both Steve and Hazel are long-time contributing editors with *The Five Stones* newsletter for small churches, which has been publishing since the 1970s. One chaired the Small Church Committee of the Troy Conference United Methodists; the other served on the National Small Church Task Force of the American Baptist Churches USA. Both have organized or co-organized regional and national small-church conventions and played key parts in drawing together various denominations' grass roots efforts to create the Small Church Movement of the 1980s, which resulted in the development of literature and other resources for small churches.

Each of us recognizes that we have filters through which we see, analyze, and articulate issues and strategies. One of us is inclined to see and describe things theologically, attitudinally, historically, and behaviorally, while the other is more likely to speak of organizational dynamics, process issues, demographics, and programmatic approaches. Our *common experiences* and shared love of the small church motivated us to undertake this project, but our *differences* have given us perspective, just as having two eyes provides the gift of depth perception.

We need to comment on how this book was written, particularly with regard to the division of labors, the writing, and the chapter format. Our styles are so different that we found it practically impossible to blend our paragraphs and sentences together. As a result, we have simply chosen to acknowledge who primarily wrote each chapter. To clarify matters for readers, we have elected to put our initials at the beginning of chapters or sections.

Last, we wanted to say a word about each other.

[SEB] "Hazel amazes me with her quiet but boundless enthusiasm for the small church. She is patient, giving, and nurturing in working with folks at small-church training events, exhibiting a style that lets people learn for themselves. And she is a terrific colleague, forever offering incisive comments, thoughtful critiques, and parallels to biblical narratives. No wonder I can never reach Hazel by phone at her home—she is in great demand with persons in her area, who are always calling her for guidance and nurture."

[HAR] "It is always a pleasure to work with Steve at small-church events. A high-energy, optimistic person, Steve brings enthusiasm and commitment to small-church issues. Even the tough issues of small-church life present Steve with the challenges of seeking new insight from biblical stories and positive approaches from other disciplines. This provides a great foundation for a team approach."

We trust the labors of our partnership will bear good fruit, and we pray our book will nourish and strengthen those who seek to raise the esteem of God's people and God's small churches.

CHAPTER I

The Little Church That Couldn't/Could

In our small church consultations and in our small church esteem workshops, we discovered that participants' *feelings* are meaningful indicators of church esteem. Emotions allow us to learn whether the congregation's health is *holistic*—deep and strong—or if the church merely appears healthy on the surface. Many low esteem congregations pretend they are high esteem churches. They are like the depressed woman who took two hours each day to dress and meticulously apply her makeup. Rather than reflecting overall fitness, her outward appearance only disguised her poor health. She spent all her energy disguising her illness instead of healing it. In like manner, many small churches seem well, but underneath the cosmetics they feel depressed and insecure as they constantly contend with a poor self-image.

When participants in one Vermont church expressed their feelings, they provided us with invaluable data. Over a period of four years, their church had gone from low esteem ("the little church that couldn't") to high esteem ("the little church that could"). One by one, individuals recalled their feelings throughout the transition.

"We felt depressed, I guess," the lay leader remarked. "Our worship attendance was down around 35-45. We wanted to blame the preachers, but the sermons weren't any better or worse than in the past."

"And we felt guilty—like it was our fault," the membership chairperson added. "No matter how hard we tried, we couldn't get any new members."

"It was next to impossible to get anyone to serve on a committee, much less chair one," a Nominations Committee member told us, "and that was very frustrating and maddening for me. It felt like people were suddenly less committed than they had been in the old days."

"When the denomination brought us candidates for a pastor, it never occurred to us to really take time to state *our* needs and truly *interview* a candidate," someone offered. "We got so desperate that we didn't feel we could afford to be selective, so we took pretty much whomever the District Superintendent sent us. We really grew passive and dependent on the denomination."

"We had no idea where we were going or what we were doing," said a middle-aged man. "All we knew was that certain things had always worked in the past, and when those things stopped working, we floundered. We collapsed."

"We stopped giving everybody keys; only the pastor and trustees had keys," said the organist. "For awhile *I* didn't even merit a key."

"That's right. I remember," interjected another woman. "It was terrible. We stopped trusting—even each other. It was like we were clutching, trying to hang on to everything."

"And anything," interrupted the middle-aged man again. "We were like a drowning man. I was a trustee then. It felt like we had to conserve, to tighten, or we'd lose it all. Somehow we voted to stop letting outside groups use our vestry. Then all our meetings—trustees meetings and all the others—ended up with us talking about shaky finances and low attendance. We were like Chicken Little, panicking because we imagined the sky was falling."

"There was *nothing* going on," someone admitted. "No activities. Just Sunday morning worship. The Sunday school even folded. The Women's Group—all older women—disbanded. The place became a cemetery."

"We hadn't fully paid our denominational apportionments or our benevolences for fifteen or twenty years," the treasurer confessed. "But at meetings, rather than allow ourselves to feel guilty about it, we felt angry—angry at the denomination for oppressing us rather than being understanding and helpful."

"I think Jesus described us when he said something about folks milling around like sheep without a shepherd," the lay leader said. "We needed some caring *and* some direction."

The membership chairperson agreed and added, "Yes, someone to help us make sense of the mess we were in. I felt stupid and uneducated. Everything was fuzzy and . . . confusing."

"I didn't even know what was going on," remarked a man in his mid-thirties. "There wasn't any real communication that I could see. I kept hearing the church cry about poverty, but I didn't know what they needed the money for. I kept hearing them beg for leaders, but I had no idea what the leaders would be doing. Someone used the word 'fuzzy', and I think that's right."

"My husband, who died last year, served on nearly every committee over the past thirty years," said a gray-haired woman. "These past ten or fifteen years he was very discouraged, though. Even when we started the recent turnaround, he couldn't fully believe it. He thought the bubble would burst at any time. It just wore him down, and he got very pessimistic."

The emotions displayed in these candid remarks make quite a list: depression, accusations, feeling guilty, at fault, frustrated, being angry at themselves, at denominations, or at non-participants. These people were exhausted. They ran on empty, strained to retrieve the past, groped along in myopia without direction, felt immobilized by the church's impotency, existed as a victimized, oppressed, passive body lacking self-determinism. They dangled feebly, almost drowning, a wary congregation that grew non-communicative, tight-fisted, selfish. The shaky nature of church life fostered disloyalty. Rendered barren and fruitless, the congregation limped along, feeling witless, uninformed, fuzzy, and dejected, finally slumping into a morass of disbelief.

Could we add more? Yes! When you merge the list of negative diminutives associated with the "small" in small church (the woeful list in our introduction), you can readily understand why so many small churches are convinced they cannot crawl out of the Pit. (The images in Psalm 30 often apply to the small church.)

In brainstorming about small church esteem, the two of us dreamed that if we had access to a motorhome and a reasonable budget, it would be interesting to conduct interviews in small churches all across North America. We would find churches from one end of the spectrum to the other. We would discover high-esteem small churches soaring on eagles' wings (especially true of new church starts). Sadly, we would also locate churches who feel as if they had stumbled into the Pit itself. Fitting into this category are the many urban "Old First" churches that have failed to recognize that the "baby boom" is over. By asking respondents not only for descriptive *information* (programs and mission), but also by inviting them to share their *feelings*, we could reasonably expect to learn much about each church's level of satisfaction and esteem.

Someone once said, "Feelings are facts; pay attention to them." It is very useful to have people talk about their church's state of health in terms of how it *feels*. The feelings provide important *descriptive* data (symptoms) that help us to form a diagnosis. From there it is possible to become *prescriptive*; with a treatment plan, we can work for change.

Those Vermont folks who were part of a low esteem church later shared what it felt like to be part of a high esteem church. We will not detail here the strategies employed to effect the turnaround. We will not highlight how they communicated, structured their board, made their decisions, organized and conducted mission and outreach, facilitated adult educational programs, recognized and appreciated their people, and related publicly. What we will emphasize right now is their *feelings*. Note the wondrous change in morale and esteem.

"We're certainly not depressed now," said the lay leader. "Our attendance at worship is at 50-65 now, quite a lot better than before. We feel better in worship, more comfortable, together and positive. We're just plain healthier and feeling better about ourselves."

"We still have committee vacancies, almost as many as before," said the Nominations Committee member, "but we've also got twice as many committees with much more program and mission activity. We've got a great many people serving—*and enjoying it*. There's so much to do. We're active now, and we all feel useful. It's like we've got direction and purpose again. Less wandering and stumbling."

"We're much more sure of ourselves," said another person. "We know we'll be losing our present pastor in a year or two—he promised us five years when he started—but you can be sure that we'll be selective about a successor. Right now we're in the midst of assessing our needs and clarifying our goals. Not just any pastor will do for this period in our church's life. We feel good enough about ourselves—after all, we're a top-notch church—that if a pastoral candidate doesn't look like a good match, we won't hesitate to speak up and ask the denomination for another—again and again if we have to. We owe it to ourselves, to the candidate, and to the denomination to strive for a healthy situation."

"The keys," interrupted the organist. "Everyone's got one. We used to keep a list of everyone who had keys, but that's out of date. I never thought about it before, but it's not the persons with keys who were a problem . . . so why did we ever limit the keys in the first place? It was really quite silly, wasn't it?"

"Even some non-members have keys now," added another woman.

"But they're responsible adults, and their groups need to get into the church. They need us."

"You're right," said a man with a deep voice. "The distrust has sort of evaporated. Cooperation seems to have chased it away. Somewhere along the line we got less possessive about the building and its contents."

If I were to paint or sculpt us as we were then and now," said a young mother, "I'd show us then in a fetal position, like a baby in the womb, with our hands crossed across our chest, protective and clutching. Now I'd show us with arms extended, reaching out, giving, instead of holding."

"Our building has become so busy with our church activities," one man said excitedly, "and with the activities of other worthwhile groups— sometimes three different church or community groups meeting the same night—that we have scheduling problems! What a blessing! Scheduling problems!"

"And financially we've turned things around. That gives us a real sense of satisfaction," said the treasurer. "We've paid all our bills, *and all our Conference Apportionments plus the Conference Benevolence*, and we've started a local benevolence program besides."

"We bought a new stove, remodeled the church kitchen, and re-placed the old furnace in the parish house," said a middle-aged woman who had become president of the rejuvenated Women's Group.

"We opened a used clothing shop two afternoons a week," said an older woman.

"It's next to the day care in our parish house," added the woman sitting beside her.

"I said we felt stupid and uneducated five or six years ago," offered the membership chairperson. "We don't feel that way any more."

Most of the people in the group nodded their heads in agreement. With spontaneity and enthusiasm, their positive comments came as rapidly as corn popping. The excitement level was rising as people got to talk about their church.

"Since those days," the membership chairperson continued, "those of us who are leaders—and there's a lot of us now—have spent many worthwhile hours in small groups, either for adult education or on committee. We've gained a better understanding of the Bible and its characters; we're more aware of missions; six or eight of us have learned lay preaching and fill in at other small churches in the area; and we've enjoyed many discussion groups together. It's all helped us feel less passive, more empowered, I think."

"Communications are better now, too. People know what's going on in our church. Members know; non-members know; the community knows. People talk about our church now, and it's not gossip; they talk about us in a good way. No wonder. We're quite a church!"

Their statements invite applause. This is clear testimony of a genuine, high esteem small church that had lived through the "Pit" experience but was now singing new songs of praise to God. The *feelings* people were describing left little doubt of this transformation.

What precipitated the turnaround, the shift from a low esteem small church to a high esteem small church? How did the symptoms and outward signs parallel the internal feelings? What attitudes and behavior had to be changed in order to accomplish this major transformation? What were the issues the congregation had to face? In the following chapters, we will address some of these questions and explore the complex issue we call *small church esteem.*

If your small church feels the despair of low esteem, use Psalm 30. God hears our genuine cries and hastens to answer. Study the Psalm using verses 4, 5, 11, 12 as a vision upon which to set your eyes. High esteem is not the result of magic but of the movement of God in the midst of a cooperating church.

CHAPTER II

What Measuring Stick for Esteem?

How do we recognize a high esteem small church? What standards of measurement would we use?

Our work with small churches suggests that a great percentage use the criteria established by the dominant culture. Society seems to endorse such concepts as "bigger is better," "climb the ladder to success," cost-effectiveness, rapid mobility, and other corporate business concepts such as management by objectives and raises linked to evaluations. These imposed values cause the small church to suffer low esteem and to operate from a survival mentality.[1] Recognizing that small congregations must live within their context, our challenge is to invite them to respond to the call of God. Often this summons entails running counter to the dominant culture.

We receive this challenge from the record of God's work with the people of Israel, through Jesus' model of behavior patterns, as well as from the story of the early church.

Our task here is to identify in small churches those qualities that are characteristic of high or low esteem. One way to assess the level of esteem is to consider churches individually. The life of a small church called Valley Queen Baptist Church in Marks, Mississippi offers clues to healthy esteem.

Valley Queen Baptist Church

Marks is a city of contrasts: wealth and poverty, employment and unemployment, the educated and the uneducated, blacks and whites. It is a city of unequal opportunity in a country that boasts of a system of justice for all. Valley Queen Baptist Church has become a beacon of hope in the midst of dejection.

From a deep commitment to Jesus, the church reaches out into the community to seek and serve a suffering humanity. Its dedicated minister, Dr. Carl Brown, extends the hand of friendship to everyone. In partnership with Dr. Brown the church builds its life on the principle that *the Good News of God's love is for the world.*

The Valley Queen Baptist Church puts dreams into action. How? Five goals push the church to give of itself to the community.

1. To eliminate hunger. Hungry people live in Marks. Their craving is not only for food; their spirit longs for friendship to dispel loneliness and faith to replace despair.

The Valley Queen Baptist Church responded to human need by becoming a "full service" church. A "full-service" church is one where worship services are held every Sunday and other programs are created to proclaim the Good News of God's love and to build community.

Hunger and loneliness are relieved through a lunch program for senior citizens. Mrs. Marjorie Brown plans nutritionally balanced meals that will feed approximately sixty persons daily, and she organizes and oversees the food preparation. Initiated by Valley Queen, expanded by American Baptist mission dollars, and recently supplemented by a grant from the American Lutherans, the meal program exemplifies how many Christians can cooperate in a ministry of hope. In addition, through church efforts, a breakfast program was started in the schools to help alleviate children's nutritional deficiencies and thus provide the nourishment needed for learning.

2. To address economic issues. Affluence and poverty are next-door neighbors—like the antebellum mansion on the hill and the shack down in its valley. While some poorer families own homes, many do not have enough money for maintenance. Some persons have frozen to death in winter while others have suffocated in summer. In response to this need, World Vision offered a grant to assist Valley Queen with its winterization projects.

Grants do not just fall into their lap; the Valley Queen pastor has vigorously sought support from numerous foundations that can reinforce the church's ministry. These monies help the church respond quickly and without undue red tape. Valley Queen has also been the catalyst for

developing a low-income apartment complex. Assisted by denominational, ecumenical, and para-church organizations, the church strives to
meet basic human needs.

3. To develop the ministry of the laity. Workshops on health
care, crime protection, the electoral process, job training and placement,
adult education, legislative and administrative advocacy equip and
enable laity to claim God's gifts.

This emphasis is enhanced through the Quitman County Development Organization (QCDO). Founded in 1976 with the aid of government programs, QCDO combats the social and economic ills of African-
Americans and other poor minorities within Quitman County, Mississippi. When government program funds were cut, the organization
faltered. However, under the leadership of Dr. Carl Brown, QCDO was
reorganized with laity empowered to lead in assuming the original
purpose of the community organization. They launched two small-scale
economic ventures—a laundromat and a clothing store. QCDO, like
Valley Queen, strives to offer people the dignity that comes with jobs,
services, and clothing.

In the summer of 1986 this ministry of the laity was extended across
ethnic lines when a group of American Baptist Indians came to participate in a Vacation Church School Program.[2] Many recall the inspiring
visit of the Native Americans from the Wichita Mission Baptist Church
of the Oklahoma Indian Baptist Association. The Indians gave some of
their signature artwork as a visual testimony proclaiming unity in Christ.

4. To educate pastoral leadership. A program to assist pastors in
developing skills has been strengthened with funds from the Ford
Foundation. Program participants are sensitized to the racial issues of
the Upper Delta Valley of Mississippi, to poverty and oppressive systems
as well as to worship in their tradition. Reinforced with hands-on experience in church and community life, pastors are being trained and
called to strengthen the ministries of other small churches. When small
plantation churches provide opportunities for pastors to practice ministry,
their church esteem is greatly enhanced.

5. To enhance esteem for children and youth. Valley Queen also
dedicates itself to the needs of children and youth. The church has a
positive relationship with the school next door; it encourages teachers

and staff to provide an atmosphere for optimal learning. The congregation itself promotes high self-esteem among youth by giving them high visibility. One Sunday the young ushers sported new uniforms. How proud they were to participate in the life of the church!

Analysis

The Valley Queen Baptist Church bears the marks of healthy small church esteem. How do we know?

Carl Dudley and Douglas Walrath, in their book *Developing Your Small Church's Potential*, address the importance of *context* on the life of the small church.[3] Valley Queen knows its context and develops its ministry in relation to it. Grants are essential to ensure program continuity and success. Many needs remain to be met, therefore, many resources need to be obtained. For this reason Dr. Carl Brown became a grant-writer.

Valley Queen functions on the *mutual ministry* theory.[4] Its pastoral team and its laity work together for the advancement of Christ's work in the world. In addition, the church cooperates with its denominational family as well as with para-church organizations. *Interdependence and partnership* are concepts that undergird the life of a high esteem church.

Vision translated into goals keeps the church focused on its mutual ministry, keeping it intentional about improving race relations. *Worship* provides vitality for church life and inspires the church to faithfulness in responding to community needs. The church knows it is making a difference by recognizing the *leadership gifts* and potential of individuals and by providing opportunity for expression of those skills. Along with the adults, children and youth are empowered.

An integral part of Valley Queen's vision is to be intentional about improving race relations. The pastor continues to cultivate cooperation with whites in the community. Some historical factors impede the full actualization of this vision at the local level. Therefore, Dr. Brown fosters positive interracial experiences for Valley Queen by inviting guests from outside the community.

Visitors to the church experience the vibrancy of its worship and express awe at the depth of its ministry. They receive the love that pours forth from the energized collaboration of pastor and people. There is the strong impression that hope is the guiding force the church channels in its relationship to the dominant culture. The church weaves its life into the prevailing issues of race, economics, employment, political endeavors, age, education, housing, and hunger. It is clear that Valley Queen stands for justice; here is a church with a voice that must be heeded.

There are ample opportunities to spread the Good News of Christ's love to one and all. At Valley Queen it is evident that dreams are encouraged, hope is fostered, education is honored, and failure is permissible.

In summary, two complementary ingredients at Valley Queen identify it as a small church soaring with self-esteem: The congregation focuses attention on its internal life and on its outward expression through social ministry. This combination is what makes the small church a dynamic spiritual force within the dominant culture. A high esteem church wins: It feels good about itself and is valued by outsiders; biblical principles serve as the guiding force.

In the real world not all small churches fit this category. Many if not most display characteristics of low esteem. We would not want to damage further a low esteem church and, because we have seen this phenomenon in too many places, the low esteem church we will examine remains nameless.

Feelslow Church, Anywhere, USA

"Tell me about your church," I asked the minister where I was invited to preach.

"The people are mostly elderly. There are usually about forty people, but it's supposed to rain, so there will only be about thirty who will be able to get out."

The sign outside the meeting house indicated the church was in a pastoral transition and was being served by an interim minister. The sanctuary, originally designed to seat five hundred, had an elevated pulpit that symbolized the importance of the preached word to the worshipping community. In the minister's study a frayed oriental rug spoke of former glory. A person could easily get a heel caught in its threadbare center. The desk and chair faced the wall in an uninviting way.

A deacon led much of the worship. Four or five children, obviously grandchildren of the church leaders, went off to church school midpoint in the service. The ornate stained glass windows not only illustrated biblical stories but also served as memorials to specific individuals in the life of the church. Alongside the windows was evidence of a leaky roof. When preaching in a church with many empty pews, it is natural to wonder about the people who had formerly worshipped there.

During the offering the "head usher" directed the two deacons as if they were a dozen. The thirty-five people looked out of place in their surroundings, but one woman in particular was noticeably restless and seemed unsure of herself. Later I learned why: She had received her eviction notice. Would she be forced to live in the streets? During the coffee hour a woman in the kitchen put extra cheese on the woman's plate, a deed that seemed to say, "At least I can give you some protein."

Hospitality, graciousness, and appreciation describe their coffee hour atmosphere. It was time to tell stories—of past glories, former wealth, and a beloved pastor who served for over two decades. One recurring comment was: "We're only a small church now, but we're like a family."

As I left, I noticed the sign advertising a thrift shop open to the public on a limited basis. This signifies the church's desire to greet people and meet the needs of a changing community.

This story is true. We have experienced this type of church countless times; surely thousands of other preachers in many denominations have encountered similar dismal settings. This true story describes too many small congregations operating today. Even though there are variations on the passing comments, they all speak of damaged esteem within the local church.

Perhaps the most common remark one is apt to hear is, "We're just a small church." The simple phrase "just a" implies low esteem. Undoubtedly many candidating pastors have been told, "You probably wouldn't be interested in us. We're not very big." This admission shows a defense mechanism at work. The small church keeps its distance in order to protect itself from rejection should a potential applicant turn down the Search Committee. Tragically, these statements become self-fulfilling prophecies.

Then there is the throat-clearing apology, "We're sorry there aren't more people here," or "Most of our people are older and can't get out any more." After a while, saying "sorry" to a host of deficiencies becomes a habit at Feelslow church.

Analysis

This is my generic description of one out of the thousands of low esteem congregations. Inward feelings as well as outward expression are indicators for both low and high esteem churches, and signs are not difficult to read.

The depression and low esteem witnessed in the Feelslow Church are typical of what we encounter in congregations once larger but now smaller (Steve refers to these as "formerly big".) Large churches that have plummeted from past glory belong to a separate category of small church and require different treatment from those that have always been small churches.

A low esteem church often suffers from remorse. There is a strong correlation with the grief process that Elisabeth Kubler-Ross identifies in five stages: denial/isolation, anger, bargaining, depression, acceptance.[5]

Denial of present realities allows a church to live in the past and behave like the larger organization it once was. Out-of-date constitutions and by-laws are perpetuated even when it is obvious there are not enough people to fill the boards.

Isolation is evidenced when a church withdraws into itself and fails to take part in its denomination or evades participation with other community churches. A church might isolate itself because it is convinced of its unworthiness. This withdrawal may be precipitated by a broken relationship with a pastor, limited finances, or some internal conflict. When a congregation does not feel good about itself, it believes it has nothing to offer.

Once *anger* emerges, the denominational personnel are often the target. The staff are *blamed* for the state of the local church, and the accusations are not difficult to imagine. "Why don't you find us a pastor who can come in here and turn this thing around?" "Why don't you give us more money so we can pay our bills?" However, anger may be aimed closer to home, directed at the "power" person or group, or the anger still might be concealed without any outward manifestation. Uncovering the anger—and its source—may prove to be extremely challenging.

Drawing the denomination into the *bargaining* arena is easy. This process usually centers around negotiating a salary package and dickering over time management: "How much time or how many services can we buy for the money we have to offer?" Or the church itself grapples with the dilemma: Should we pay the oil bill or the minister?

"Down in the dumps" accurately describes the feeling of *depression*. There is nothing lower than rock bottom; from there, the way to the top looks insurmountable. Memories become more painful with each re-collection; even the positive force of the church's history diminishes.

Many churches never arrive at *acceptance* of the new state of being; some die on the vine. However, a church that realizes the possibility of starting over can create a new identity which fits its new situation. A church with a clear identity will have a new vision for ministry.

The feelings of a low esteem church may be compared to the feelings of the homeless. A study of homelessness shows major similarities: loss of identity, work, and home; prevailing sense of bewilderment; an impression of being victimized; and an existence in an atmosphere of hopelessness, despair, and powerlessness.[6] Worry and anxiety sap the spirit; all energy is spent on survival.

From the story of the once-large-now-small church, many factors indicate low church esteem. Among them are those behavior patterns that clearly reveal an identity crisis. Examination of the operating structure at this time will usually show vacancies on boards and committees. Budget restraints become the order of the day even in a church with a large endowment. When the church uses the adjective small, it is now referring to *numbers* rather than to *identity*—the modifier is diminutive rather than descriptive.

An identity crisis leaves a church unclear about its mission and its purpose.[7] The inward focus on comfort and survival becomes unprofitable and only perpetuates the downward cycle.[8] The church's life becomes a "once-upon-a-time story."

In contrast, if the church attempts to reclaim lost esteem or to seek a fresh identity, then it can move forward and respond to new openings for ministry."[9]

When a person loses a job, an identity crisis arises. Friends disappear; bills mount; the home crumbles. In a similar way, when a church loses its identity and turns inward, community status topples. With its unclear and weakened role, the congregation no longer influences those outside its realm. In some communities church life has become so inward people cannot even give directions to the church building. It has become a nonentity in its own back yard! However, even in the story of the once larger church, the mission connection still expresses itself through the thrift shop. Even in its decline, the congregation can continue to reach out into the community.

Proof of low church esteem is seen in the building itself. Tight finances prohibit repairs and satisfactory housekeeping. A musty smell permeates the building because the facility is closed more than it is opened. As the paint fades, darkness settles in, literally and figuratively. With limited funds, the thermostat must be set at low temperatures. No longer is there money to pay a sexton, and the aging congregation's physical energy dwindles as they look at the building's overwhelming maintenance needs. The church looks unkempt and gives the appearance that its people are stingy.

Another major indicator of low esteem is the loss of a full-time pastor, however, the congregation will probably expect any part-timer who assumes the job to do the work of a full-time pastor. The church continues to weaken as it loses the generational span within the church family. The congregation has lost its vigor as an effective force in community life.

Summary

These two examples reveal that leadership, finances, buildings, community needs, and vision influence small church esteem. Though these stories feature certain aspects of high and low esteem in small churches, each congregation remains unique. As you read further in this book you may discover other things that seem to describe some aspect of your church life. Make opportunities for your church to discuss and reflect, for this will provide the grist for being intentional about your church life.

For Discussion and Reflection

1. Use the ASSESSMENT GRID on page 17 to help your church discover its morale level.

2. What can your church do to project a positive image to the community? Identify at least one community need to which your church can and will respond.

3. Identify ways in which your church adopts newcomers into its life.

4. How does your church encourage its members to use their gifts?

5. How does participation with other churches energize your church?

Assessment Grid[10]

This instrument can help you to compile "feeling" data about your church. Use it with a group or the church itself. After each person has marked the scale, gather the results. Total the points for the first item and divide by the number of members participating to produce the average. Repeat the procedure for each item on the list. Use the results to determine "low" areas for the church to address and "high" areas for the church to affirm.

High Morale	5 4 3 2 1	**Low Morale**
Positive and optimistic	5 4 3 2 1	Negative and pessimistic
People feel cared about	5 4 3 2 1	People feel uncared for
Good relationship with pastor	5 4 3 2 1	Poor relationship with pastor
Competent, caring leaders	5 4 3 2 1	Incompetent, uncaring leaders
Participation is a joy	5 4 3 2 1	Participation is a duty
Visitors are welcomed	5 4 3 2 1	Visitors are endured
People trust one another	5 4 3 2 1	People seek hidden motives
Stress theology of grace	5 4 3 2 1	Stress theology of judgment
Active in community	5 4 3 2 1	Withdrawn from community
Well known in community	5 4 3 2 1	Unknown in the community
Atmosphere warm, bright	5 4 3 2 1	Atmosphere cold and drab
Can pay their way	5 4 3 2 1	Fear of red ink
Conflict is handled	5 4 3 2 1	Conflict is hidden
High mission commitment	5 4 3 2 1	Low mission commitment
Review successes	5 4 3 2 1	Recall mainly defeats
Open to different ideas	5 4 3 2 1	Resist innovations
Faith is joyous	5 4 3 2 1	Faith is dutiful
Active with denomination	5 4 3 2 1	Inactive with denomination
Work with local churches	5 4 3 2 1	Does not work with local churches
Hopeful about future	5 4 3 2 1	Anxious about future
Visible appreciation	5 4 3 2 1	Take people for granted

CHAPTER III

Does Size Make a Difference?

In small church workshops I find it useful—not just for newcomers but for *experienced* lay and clergy persons—to offer a thumbnail sketch of church dynamics. This helps people comprehend the organism with which they work. When shared in a small church setting (e.g., a weekend "identity assessment"), this overview seems to reduce tensions between some church members and tends to smooth out a few underlying conflicts. Often for the first time people find themselves able to share a common concept and speak the same language. This is most evident when folks from large and small congregations, from urban and rural settings, find themselves suddenly thrust together in the same church.

Why is it important to grasp how size affects the church? Simply this: Congregations that vary in size function differently. I see the small church as an *organism* and the large church as an *organization*. As a result, participants' behavior is relative to and appropriate for the size of the organism or organization. There are distinct ways of making decisions ranging from consensus to participatory democracy, and, as numbers increase, to a representative democracy. Imagine making decisions around the family dinner table, then trying to apply that method to a country of 240 million people.

To facilitate decision and policy making and in order to accomplish tasks, governing boards and committees need restructuring, expansion, or, in some cases, reduction. One organizational chart does not fit all sizes. The need for scheduling and planning increases along with organizational growth and activities. Modes of communication change. Informal, verbal communication may work well in an organism, but with expansion to organization size, communication will be primarily formal and written. Evangelism, member replacement, attraction and assimilation of newcomers, stewardship, and other group maintenance functions all change with size.

At least they *should change* with size. They should change with size *as appropriate*. This is not always the case. A growing church might find itself on a plateau it cannot seem to surmount. A church that has experienced shrinkage may be frustrated in trying to operate with a governing structure that leaves the faithful remnant wearing too many hats. They find themselves struggling to assign names to functionally defunct committees just to satisfy the system's paperwork.

As a consultant I often see churches of one size operating (or trying to operate) with systems and processes suitable for a different size church. One frequent symptom is the friction produced when some— usually newcomers—assume decisions are made one way; in practice they learn that the opposite is true. Often I find that the decision-making processes of two or three different size organizations are all trying to operate at the same time.

Imagine, if you will, that the skills you have for understanding and operating in a group are those you learned in a family. Suddenly you find yourself beamed down into a large corporation equipped with flow charts, subcommittees, and long-range planning sessions. Throughout the company and among the people a strong sense of anonymity prevails. That may be what it feels like for some small church folks who find themselves in a large church. The verbal, visual, and organizational cues and the modes of operating, reporting, and relating differ greatly from what they have learned works in a small setting. What proved successful in the family-sized organization no longer works. No wonder they feel lost, disconnected, homesick, embarrassed, shunned, and devalued.

The converse is also true. A person familiar only with large organizations will feel equally adrift if he or she responds to a highly relational and informal organism by using corporate cues and behavior. By way of analogy we can grasp what it is like for individuals from large churches to try to function in small churches by relying only on large-system skills.

Given society's demographic shifts (rural to urban, urban to rural, large to small and vice versa), along with the breakdown of denominational lines and loyalties, is it not understandable that conflicts exist in churches today? These are not merely clashes of values, theologies, and polities; there are also *conflicting systems of operation*. The basic reason is that church members have not been helped to comprehend *together* the organism or organization to which they presently belong, both or all of which are called "church."

Consider, too, that pastors are not interchangeable. Each brings his or her values and histories, be they from urban, suburban, or rural backgrounds. Personality types and temperaments vary. How comfortable they feel in different parishes will affect their leadership success or failure.

Similarly, many pastors will function better in one size church than in another. A few versatile pastors efficiently manage almost any size church. However, that is partially because they honed different skills and adapted the necessary behavior for surviving and thriving in each particular size organization.

Most pastors don't seem to be that versatile. A majority seems generally to function better in one size rather than in another. There are multiple reasons why pastors move through different-size church pastorates, including financial need, status and advancement, variety and new challenges, power needs, loneliness, or sheer boredom. However, *very seldom do pastors pay attention to, or base their decision on, the comfort factor associated with organizational size.* What a radical thought! This idea suggests that we not choose a church or ministry based on the dominant culture's or even the denomination's standards for success. Instead, are we to regard church size and focus on how comfortable, competent, and faithful we feel when we operate in it?

Consider this. What are the consequences of a good, small church pastor "climbing the ladder" of success, moving to larger and larger churches? Do some pastors perform according to the "Peter Principle"? And how does our disparate pay scale affect the distribution of pastors among various size churches? Does the compensation structure encourage the Peter Principle? Does this foster mismatches that bring inevitable conflict and forced terminations?[1]

We must begin to take seriously the importance of an organization's size, for if we mismatch size and systems—communications, decision making, pastoral selection, governance, group maintenance—it will very likely lead to conflict, dysfunction, and organizational paralysis of the local Body of Christ.

The following is a conceptual framework that is most likely unknown to many clergy and laity. Workshop participants often say it helps them return to their work in the small church with a clearer vision. It is not unusual to hear someone make a correlation: "For a year now I've been a Program Church pastor in a Family Church, trying to turn a cat into a garden!"

The size-related models of Arlin Rothauge (Family, Pastoral, Program, and Corporation Church) have been around for about a decade, though they have not received the exposure they deserve.[2]

Lyle Schaller's analogies of the cat, collie, garden, house, and mansion are valuable, easy-to-visualize working models.[3] Schaller's organic pictures that use familiar—and sometimes funny—images are predicated on a numerical base similar to Rothauge's. In fact, Schaller and Rothauge complement each other quite nicely. Seeing Rothauge's *size models* on paper illustrated with Schaller's tangible, "real life" *images*—cat, collie, garden—enables people to grasp more clearly how things work. They begin to see how the *systems* (decision making, planning, member assimilation), *functions*, and *roles* (matriarch, patriarch, chaplain, gatekeeper) all adjust as *size* changes.

The Family Church (2-35 at worship)[4]

Rothauge refers to the smallest of his models—those congregations with 0-50 active members—as "The Family Church." We modify this (and the other size models) by using *average attendance at worship* rather than the number of active members, preferring that the Family Church be described as averaging 2-35 at the principal weekly worship service.

The Family Church may be part of a "circuit" or "multiple-point charge" (i.e., the second, third, or fourth in a field of churches served by one pastor), or it exists alone. However, this type of congregation is generally served by a part-time pastor who is a bivocational, "tentmaker" pastor working another (often secular) job, or an individual who offers less than a full-time resident pastor because of service demands from other churches in a field. There are even more possibilities. The congregation may be served by a lay person; by a licensed or certified lay speaker/preacher; by a retired, ordained clergyperson; by a succession of "pulpit supply" persons (lay and clergy, depending on availability); or even by a student minister who commutes to the parish and performs pastoral duties in the Family Church. Frequently a "preach-and-run"

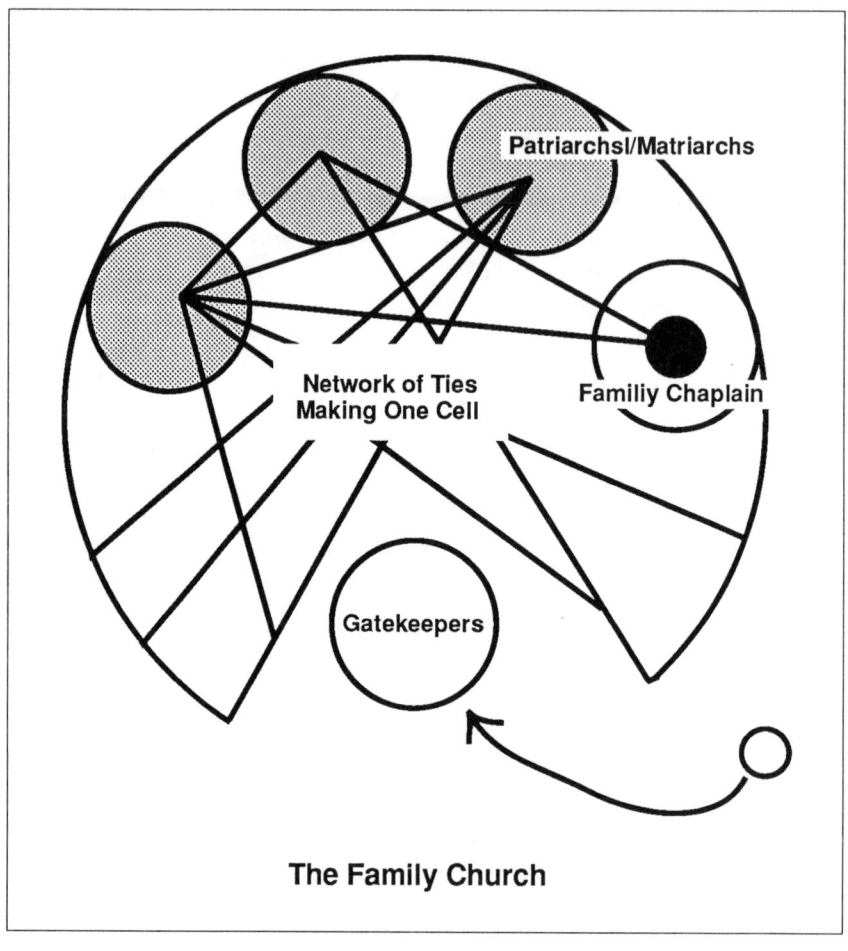

The Family Church

commuting nonresident attends to the Family Church. There are, of
course, exceptions, but the point is: *the Family Church is seldom served
by a full-time resident minister.* While some are located in a smattering
of urban centers and small towns, Family Churches are mainly situated in
rural areas.

Because of the part-time nature of the pastorate in the Family
Church, the preacher's capacity and functions are limited and more like
those of a military or institutional *chaplain* than "the leader" and resident
"vision-bearer," as is commonly the pastor's role in churches larger than
the Family Church.

The chaplain analogy fits well. A chaplain in a military unit or a hospital marries, baptizes, buries, visits, leads worship, counsels, and performs some of the administrative work. However, he or she generally is not considered "the leader" because the congregation is not handled as a forward-moving organizational entity. The vision for a military unit comes from its secular leaders and not from the chaplaincy. There is a correlation between chaplains and Family Church leadership. While the pastor performs tasks and functions, he or she is not a full participant and resident member of the localized community of faith.

The uncertainty of this leadership role translates into a high turnover rate. As a result, the person serving as pastor is likely to be regarded as only one leader among many; he or she will not be valued as *the* key leader. Or the pastor might be treated as a special visitor whose service is helpful but not indispensable to the Family church. In some situations, even if a preach-and-run pastor is in and out, the "family chaplain" might be a lay person (elder) who is affirmed by the faith community, even though he or she does not preach.[5] In effect, the pastoral role may be divided between two or among three persons.

Not only does the Family Church *feel* like family to its participants, in some instances, the church literally is family. Especially in rural areas, congregations frequently consist of families or clans. Bonds between families are further strengthened through intermarriage.

The Family Church is a *relational* entity, functioning as an organism rather than as an organization. The congregation's power base will most likely be determined *by position in the clan or in the cluster of families rather than by elected office.* Titles such as Board Chairperson, Committee Chair, or Delegate to Annual Conference will most likely be related to *tasks to be performed to satisfy the organizational requirements* of such outside groups as the Conference, District, Association, or denomination. These imposed titles might have little connection with the power needed to effect change on the local church or community level. In this relational structure authority is given *to people* rather than to positions or offices.

The dynamics are easier to understand in terms of *roles* and *functions* important to the organism itself. Accordingly, old Mr. Smith is a *patriarch*—not necessarily beloved or even aged, but esteemed, honored, and authorized by the group to assume the lead. Without his wink or nod of approval a major decision will not be made. If neither patriarch Smith nor *matriarch* Mrs. Bisset—past President of the Women's Guild—are present when consideration is given to a major decision, the process comes to a standstill. The governing board will talk around in circles until the next meeting *because of the need for the nod before proceeding.* (I am not saying this is right or wrong; this is just the way it is.)

The concept of role-taking also appears in the way newcomers are assimilated. Newcomers are either born into the congregation, marry or are adopted into it. They may be treated as *tolerated visitors,* or they may never be accepted into the fold. The process of assimilation may become a strenuous effort of proving oneself. During that time the organism's *gatekeepers* (assumed roles rather than elected positions) are responsible for introducing the newcomer to the church community *and particularly to the matriarchs and patriarchs* for inspection. The gatekeepers' roles may even mean to *hold* the newcomer in the organism long enough for the matriarch(s) and patriarch(s) to finally approve of the individual. As in an extended family, if the newcomer is not truly accepted by at least one of the family leaders, that person will probably never be allowed full participation and privileges.

In the Family Church decisions are primarily made by *consensus.* While not everyone might say yes, each one agrees *not to say no,* for one negative would block the entire process. In larger Family Churches and other moderate-size congregations, especially during times of conflict— and frequently with a split ensuing—decision by consensus may be replaced by a *participatory democracy.* It is not unusual then, in the Family Church, to have a decision voted by the majority that somehow *never gets acted upon*—because the matriarch or patriarch didn't vote with the majority. The rule "one person, one vote" does not always apply here, just as it may not in a family, tribe, or clan. Votes are weighted in a relational society such as the Family Church.

The key to understanding the small church with 2-35 at worship is to recognize that it is a *single-cell relational organism* that operates most like an extended family, clan, or tribe. Its decision making, power and authority structures, role-taking, assimilation of newcomers, and interrelationship of participants—including the pastor—are unique and size-related.

Lyle Schaller compares this size church to a *cat.*[6] It is a single organic unity (the head of the cat doesn't go far without the tail). No one really *owns* a cat, though many of us think we do; it is more true that the cat owns us and gets us to do its bidding. Like the cat, the Family Church is self-contained, self-sufficient, resourceful, and independent. And it can be ornery. If the owner (pastor) leaves for vacation, the cat manages to get its needs met. In fact, it may not even acknowledge that the owner is away. It is next to impossible for the cat owner (pastor) to teach the pet cat tricks. Tenacious, cat-like, Family Churches can survive neglect, abuse, and a steady flow of new owners—they endure. With nine lives and a knack for landing on their feet, these cat-like congregations with 2-35 at worship—by the grace of God—keep going.

The Pastoral Church (35-90 at worship)[7]

Rothauge refers to the next size church as the Pastoral Church. He defines it as having 50-150 active members; we suggest it is the congregation that averages 35-90 in attendance. As its name suggests, the church is a relational society or organism usually operating around a solo pastor. Though there are always exceptions, pastors in these model congregations serve more than half-time and reside in the community. Rothauge states that "the pastoral church finds it needs more cohesive leadership due to the increase of size over and against the more intimate one-cellular structure."[8]

We would disagree slightly here, arguing that the Pastoral Church, though not quite as intimate as the Family Church, *is nevertheless a single-celled organism* in which everyone either knows everyone else or knows about them. *Organizationally*, the church with 35-90 at worship operates in a single-cell manner—most often as a participatory democracy. The people generally try to attend most of the church's fellowship, educational, and fundraising functions. While this model can include two or three cells of intense relationships that are *superimposed* on one another, this size congregation is not yet truly multi-celled. The Pastoral Church will only evidence some multi-cell characteristics at the upper numerical end.

The usual setting for this size church is the town or the suburb. A small ethnic or "mission" church, particularly one supported by the denomination, will probably be served by a full-time resident pastor, even though the congregation has less than thirty-five at worship. Despite its low numbers, this type of church would operate under a Pastoral

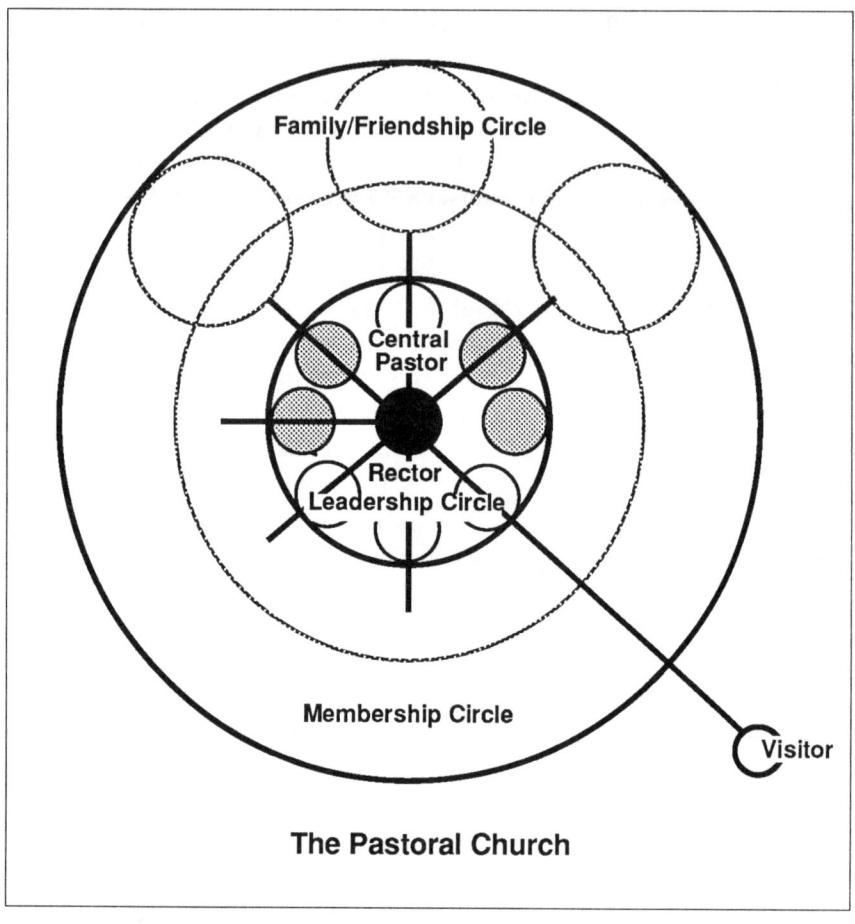

Family/Friendship Circle

Central Pastor

Rector Leadership Circle

Membership Circle

Visitor

The Pastoral Church

rather than Family Church model. This is, however, an exception to the Rothauge paradigms.

In the Pastoral Church, matriarchs and patriarchs will still exert some influence when deciding important issues, but their power is lessened. Instead, a leadership circle develops, headed by a paid professional minister who assumes the role of *chief* Patriarch or *chief* Matriarch. Both the leadership circle and the membership in general look to this central leader for "direction, inspiration, and pastoral care." This leader will still be able to maintain close personal relationships with most of the members of the Pastoral Church, but because of the size of this unwieldy single-cell organism and its organizational needs, a hierarchy emerges.

Because it *appears* that belonging means relating closely to the clergyperson, newcomers must get attention from the minister soon if they are to become members. The gatekeeper is often replaced in the Pastoral Church by a greeter and a Guest Book or Visitor's Log. Then the clergyperson is expected to follow up and begin a relationship with the newcomer. Sometimes designated lay persons will initiate the first visit and hold the newcomer until the pastor can start a relationship. In such cases they perform as gatekeepers do in the Family Church. The growth limitation is obvious: Church size depends on the number of relationships the clergyperson can establish and maintain.

Schaller nicknames this Pastoral Church the "collie."[9] Like the "cat" congregation, the collie congregation is a unity: its head does not go anywhere without its tail. Unlike the cat, the collie is more dependent on its master for regular feeding and care. However, the collie can be taught a few tricks.

Pastors generally view collie churches as more receptive and willing to adopt new ideas. These same leaders will get frustrated at the resistance they face when suggesting new ideas to cat churches. Collies and their masters are mutually affectionate. When the pastor returns from a three-week vacation, the collie congregation will respond with devotion and effusiveness: "So glad you're back! No, we didn't have the Bible study group while you were gone—not without you!" No matter how great the pulpit-supply person was during the master's absence, no one gets too excited or even comments on the replacement's sermons. Many pastors feel very affirmed, loved, and comfortable in the collie-like Pastoral Church. As long as they provide the direction, inspiration, and shepherding care their congregation needs, the affection and appreciation will continue.

Because of the single-cell nature of the Family Church and the Pastoral Church, we consider both models *small churches*. Occasionally we discover a single-cell church with 250 members rather than the figure of 200 many denominations prefer when defining what constitutes a small church. Or, we might find a single-cell congregation with approximately one hundred at worship. While the church does not expand to the next size, it comfortably maintains its numbers. Despite not fitting the numerical guidelines, their single-cell nature identifies them as *small churches.* Conversely, we have seen churches with seventy-five at worship operating like *medium-sized churches.* In these cases, it is the *single-cell characteristic* of the congregations and *not their numbers* that identifies them as small churches. However, when we refer to the small church in our workshops or in this text, we basically refer to Family and Pastoral Churches.

Having said that, there is one more model we need to introduce.

The Program Church (90-150 at worship)[10]

The next size church, which Rothauge identifies as having 150-350 active members, is the Program Church. We prefer identifying it as having 90-150 at worship. Because of its *multi-cell nature,* division of labor, and variety of programs, Schaller nicknames it "the garden."[11] You can join the corn [the choir] while never knowing the peas [adult Bible class] or the spinach [parenting class]. In this model, the pastor's role changes. Generally, he or she relates to the leadership circle and various committees and sub-committees, and often assumes the responsibility for training and equipping a cadre of leaders. Once instructed and delegated, leaders direct programs. In this model, the pastor is less likely to be *the* primary leader, which is foundational to the Pastoral Church model. By sheer volume of people involved, the pastor will be limited in developing and maintaining close, personal relationships with the entire congregation.

An intimate, single-cell Pastoral Church that is just starting to grow numerically into an activities-oriented, multi-cell organization (Program Church) will often hear grumbling: "We don't know each other any more; we never see the pastor any more; he or she hardly ever stops to visit and socialize." In this scenario, growth means dealing with an identity crisis because suddenly "we're sensing we're not who we always knew we were."[12] (This is descriptive of the plateau experienced by the church trying to get above 90-110 at worship.)

Participants will experience some sense of intimacy and "small-churchness" in the sub-groups, such as the longstanding senior choir or the adult Sunday school class that has been together 10-20 years. These cells may function as a Family Church, complete with chaplain, matriarchs, patriarchs, and gatekeepers. However, the congregants generally

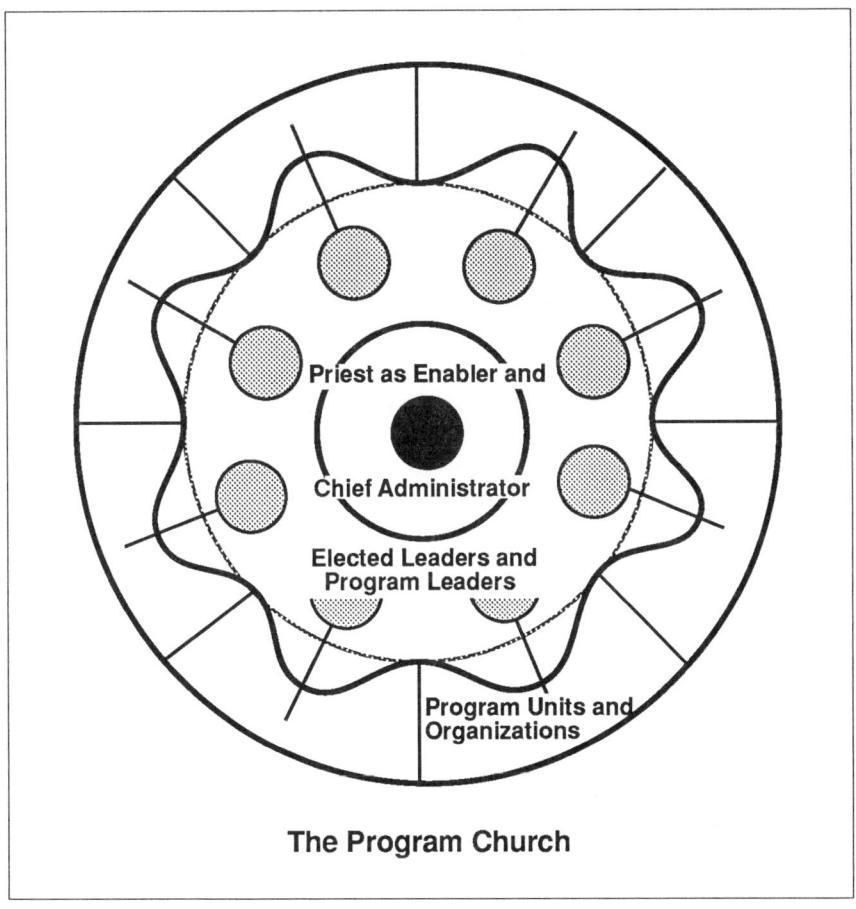

Priest as Enabler and Chief Administrator

Elected Leaders and Program Leaders

Program Units and Organizations

The Program Church

find the *entire* congregation no longer operates as a single-cell small church.[13] Representative democracy must replace participatory democracy. Programming, complicated by facility and leadership scheduling and the allocation of equipment and resources, requires longer time frames, more committee work, and the delegation of duties. Because the church is more program-oriented, newcomers are likely to be attracted to the quality, availability, and variety of programs. For them, the atmosphere of an "extended family" might have little appeal, except in the sub-group they choose to join. Understandably, a program-attraction model of evangelism and assimilation is more common in the Program Church model. This is far different from the manner in which newcomers enter and join the Family (birth, marriage, adoption) and Pastoral (relationship with pastor) Churches.

Many churches vacillate between the Pastoral and the Program models. With population surges or the tenure of a popular pastor, congregations find themselves expanding and contracting. Every couple of years the church is caught in the throes of an identity crisis and is unable to recognize the pattern. Isn't that what esteem is about—knowing who we are and claiming that identity? There are behavioral, structural, relational, governmental, and manifold other changes that accompany the move from one size church to another. Failure to address these challenges consequently leads to a diminishing of church esteem.

For Discussion and Consideration

1. Which size church are you *numerically* (number in worship)?

2. What size church do your *characteristics* and ways of operating suggest you are?

3. How do *newcomers* enter your church? How do they get "glued in"?

4. How do you make decisions? By *consensus*? (Even though not everyone fully agrees, no one disagrees strongly enough to stop the group from approving an idea.) By *participatory democracy*? (Everyone has a vote and clearly gets a chance to speak up. Yet it is the governing board, known to most of the people, who facilitates the decisions regarding the church's day-to-day operations, even though policy issues are often debated and voted on by everyone.) By *representative democracy*? (Elected representatives make policy, draft plans, organize programs, etc., shifting toward communication feedback from members as written or survey data.) By *a combination of these methods*?

5. Do you fluctuate between sizes? What are the contributing factors for this? Leadership changes? Population shifts? Crises and conflicts?

6. Do some of your members *perceive* you as one size church while others perceive you as another? Are those perceptions due to members' experience elsewhere, a change in your church's size and way of operating (decision making, programming, worship, leadership), or other factors?

7. With members having different perceptions about your church's size and identity, how does this shape their *expectations*? Of the pastor's time and priorities? Of your programs, outreach, evangelism, and member assimilation?

8. Seeing that the pastor's *role* may differ in the three church models, how does that apply to you when you seek pastoral leadership? How will the varying roles affect the way you look at resumes or profiles? How will you structure your interviews, and what will you hope to discover about the person?

9. If you do not act according to your size (e.g., a Family or a Pastoral Church trying to staff and offer programs suited to the resources of a Program Church), what happens to your church esteem? How do you deal with your sense of failure? Blame? Abandonment? Tentativeness? ("We tried it before, and it didn't work, so why ever try it again?")

10. How can you discover or adapt what is appropriate for your size church in its particular context in order to *raise* your church esteem? Worship? Programs? Mission and outreach?

CHAPTER IV

Leadership and Small Church Esteem

The nature of the small church described in the previous chapter has implications for its leadership. Here several relationships will be considered that affect a congregation's esteem. We will discuss community, local church, pastors, interim ministers, denominations, and seminaries.

The Community

Since its inception the church has existed within a community, such as the New Testament congregations located in Jerusalem, Corinth, and Ephesus. Today small churches exist within metropolitan, suburban, or rural communities. Each local church is called to live out its ministry in some particular setting, most often under the guidance of a pastor.

A local church seems most conscious of its surrounding community during the interim when a pastoral search is conducted or when it is involved in an intentional assessment process. The people examine the community's expectation of the church as well as ministry, the services the church offers in the community.

It is a reality that some or many constituents travel to church activities from outside the immediate area. As a result, the church with many commuting members is largely ignorant about the surrounding neighborhood. The tendency is not to invest in the church's community.

The search for an appropriate pastor will be influenced by the perceived ministry needs of the larger community. Frequently African-American churches expect a pastor to be involved in community affairs, hoping to influence political structures toward justice. The Hispanic community's need for expert social service skills will be listed in that church's criteria for pastoral selection.

In some communities small churches isolate themselves from the fabric of their community, a negative behavior that will affect the church's self-understanding as well as the pastor's role. Rapid changes in urban, small town, and rural communities make newcomers feel uneasy. They fear anticipated differences in lifestyle and value systems. Yet even in these situations a community frequently will entertain high expectations of church leaders.

Communities often look to the church for something even when it is unclear what that something is. When there is a traumatic death in a community people automatically look to the church for comfort, how-ever, when life seems smooth and uneventful, people tend to neglect the church. High-esteem small churches have a high profile in the commu-nity, whereas low-esteem small churches often have a low profile in the community.

The Church

The quality of local church life affects the small church's projected image and influences how outsiders are invited to participate. Hints of the esteem level appear most clearly in the transition time between pastors.

The following quotes aide our understanding of how a leadership gap influences both community ministry and church life.

"You won't stay here very long; no one ever stays here."

"We'll just get you trained and then you'll leave us."

"You wouldn't be interested in coming here, you're looking for a bigger place."

"We can't afford to pay very much."

These statements reflect low esteem. One can read between the lines the passivity in accepting the unacceptable. The people long for intimacy, but out of a defense mechanism they build walls to protect themselves from hurt and disappointment.

Many small churches live with a pastoral change occurring every three to five years. Some small churches acquiesce, assuming this is the way it is, the way it always has been, and the way it always will be. This attitude defeats churches and exacerbates low esteem. However, others believe the ministry of their small church is to train pastors, and they beam with pride at the accomplishments of pastors who began their ministries with them. This perspective is especially true for small churches that accommodated student pastors during seminary years.

The time between pastors stresses the small congregation, causing apprehension among its emotionally frayed members. Interims conjure up good and bad memories connected with calling a new minister.

Some small churches, perhaps unconsciously and out of fear, alter their behavior after an extended pastor-parish relationship. The pastor might interpret this attitude shift as a cue to move on. Some pastors whose personal and professional self-esteem may be unsteady cannot discern when a church is testing the pastor's love and care. The real question may be: "Will you still love the church even when it is unlovable?" or "Are you going to take off as soon as all the rest have?" New behavior patterns need to be developed in order to nurture long-term relationships. After four or five years, many pastors have emphasized, "I'm really just getting to know the people and the people are just now beginning to trust me."

In addition, the small church may be plagued by an accumulation of disappointments with its previous ministers. Bearing the scars of mismatches, the people cringe at the memory of those desperate candidates who seemingly accepted their small church pastorates as a last resort. But this can work both ways. The church can act rashly out of its own sense of insecurity, as aptly expressed in Walter Cook's title *Send Us a Minister . . . Any Minister Will Do.*[1]

Whether impatient to secure a pastor or pestered into action by denominational leaders, a congregation might carelessly choose an ineffective pastor. This is sad. With patience and prudence the church could have identified the individual with the appropriate qualities for small church ministry in its unique context, be that the challenge of metropolitan, suburban, or rural ministry.

Another mitigating factor is a poor closure process related to the previous pastor's departure. Unresolved grief or guilt can often hamper the future ministry of a pastor and a church. There is never a good time to leave; there is no easy way to bid goodbye to people one has come to know intimately and to love deeply.

There are steps to take that can help both the church and the pastor.

The denominational staff may be approached to conduct an exit interview and to help with the creation of a worship service that acknowledges the breaking of pastoral ties and communicates future behavior patterns. A farewell "roast" and time of fellowship could be organized. In those situations involving a rift in the relationship, so much secrecy clouds the event that no one quite understands what has happened. In the aftermath, the former pastor's name is barely mentioned in what seems like an attempt to wipe those months or years from the record. A better approach might be to ask: What have we learned from this experience that will help us in the future? The practice of worship services focusing on repentance, forgiveness, and God's mercy will help churches and pastors through this difficult time.

These realities in the life of the small church enhance or impede the pastor-people relationship and affect the small church's esteem.

The Pastor

A primary relationship in the small church is the one developed with its pastor. Carl Dudley used the image of "lover" to help the small church understand pastor-people relations.[2] I am proposing the image of *companion*. A companion implies the relationship of a helpful friend, someone who walks with another person in the celebrations and challenges of life. A fitting synonym is "partner."

This image is based on Jesus' call to the disciples as described in Mark 3:14, in which Jesus appointed the twelve "to be with him" (NRSV). My experience indicates that small churches seek in their pastor a person who will accompany them in the joys and sorrows of life. The companionship model of ministry lends itself well to small church work that is accomplished out of a sense of belonging, an attitude that says "we're in this thing together." Struggles are shared in common as are the joys of life. This is the relationship suggested by Paul to the Corinthian church: "If one member suffers, all suffer together with it; if one member is honored, all rejoice together with it" (1 Corinthians 12:26 NRSV).

Rooted in love, the pastor-people relationship is strengthened through daily interactions. This bonding of pastor and people provides the foundation for spiritual development and outreach. Based on unconditional love that seeks and wants the best for all, companionship becomes a testimony to the "more excellent way" described by Paul (1 Corinthians 13). Solid fellowship, maintained through worship and spiritual development, means that the church can do the work it is called to do. That work, based on Jesus' call to his disciples, is "to be sent out to proclaim the message, and to have authority to cast out demons" (Mark 3:14c, 15 NRSV). Companionship is the impetus that causes the small church to concentrate on what it does best, namely, telling stories of God's love in action and living the life of deep caring for the needs of others.

The companionship model of ministry is enhanced by a minister-church covenant that is developed to clarify expectations. Though covenants have often tended to focus on common understandings regarding time and finances (more like contracts), the trend today is to encourage both parties to pay attention to the work expectations.

The first purpose is to openly communicate expectations, both reasonable and perhaps unrealistic. Nevertheless, it must be recognized that some people's expectations might not be formulated and remain unspoken. Only after the pastor's arrival will these additional wishes emerge. For instance, a common assumption is that the pastor is the one to adjust the thermostat for Sunday worship.

The second purpose for a covenant is to list concrete expectations as a standard of measure in order to better appraise the pastor's performance. This work can help the church know what it has accomplished and when it needs to address new goals required through the maturing companionship. As pastor and people work together, priorities are altered, some omitted, others added. A working covenant prevents the pastor and the people from functioning with only one set of expectations during the entire pastoral tenure.

Covenants are not new to the life of the church. In fact, the covenant concept has a long biblical history. God made covenants with leaders in Israel, with the early church, as well as with the universal church established through Jesus Christ (the "New Covenant").

Even in places where there is resistance to the formalized agreement, there is still a covenant relationship; however, this is based on expectations that are assumed rather than articulated. Furthermore, covenants can enhance church esteem because they provide the mutual understanding essential for a healthy pastor-people relationship.

The main ingredients for high small church esteem include healthy intra-church relations; a strong, trusting pastor-people relationship founded on a clear covenant; and an obvious connection with the surrounding community. There are other influential factors contributing to small church esteem that we will now explore: denominations, interim ministers, and the seminaries.

The Denomination

Critical to high esteem in small churches is the denomination's attitude toward the congregation's life and ministry. The biblical model of companionship is probably the most effective model for denominational staff to adopt in working with small churches.

While companionship is developed in a variety of ways, it is primarily built on attitudes. Small churches need to know they are valued for who they are and for what they can contribute to Christ's church and ministry in the world. Affirmation creates an atmosphere for bonding.

Because denominational staff have sometimes accepted a small church's self-perception as "second class," "first class" treatment has not been offered. A self-deprecatory attitude suggests, "We don't deserve much and don't expect much," to which the *denominational* attitude responds, "You don't deserve much, so don't expect much." This negative attitude slices like a two-edged sword. Second-class churches crave first-class treatment, but never dare to expect it. This disposition is hardly a biblical norm; instead it is influenced by societal, business, and bureaucratic standards. David Ray's interpretation of the biblical record indicates that God elevates the *small*—the least of the tribes of Israel, the leaven in the loaf.[3] Society, with its efficiency models, has led us to believe that bigger is better. Dispelling the negative views often linked to the small church is elementary to the building of companionship between denominational staff and the congregation.

In small churches with high turnover, pastoral leadership change is commonly understood by denominational staff as prime time for renewal. This interim time offers tremendous opportunity for developing companionship between denominational staff and the small church. A church is particularly vulnerable during transitions, and may be experiencing grief over the loss of its last pastor. Losing its leader may have pushed the church to face its financial realities along with other issues such as the implications of mobility in the congregation with migrating retired folks, the loss of participants suggesting restructuring, and the challenge of a commuter congregation.

There is another perspective, and that is one of great possibility. The interim time can be a "safe" time in which to experiment. It is time to learn or relearn the church's story, integrate new members more fully into the life of the church, identify new opportunities for ministry, and work with people or events that might generate fresh opportunities for ministry. It is a time for the denomination to work with the shadow side of church life as the church learns new ways of relating.

The denomination's attitude toward the small church's pastoral change process is often hampered by a wrong posture and too many demands. Small churches are often branded as *marginal*, perceived as meager, poorly funded ministries going nowhere. Sometimes small churches are believed to be self-serving, and this conviction becomes the excuse for the denominational pastoral placement person to reduce her or his time commitment. This curtailed involvement reflects the denomination's low expectations and mental marginalization of the small church. This obviously will hamper the staff's ability to be a companion, especially in the prerequisite self-study process in the pastoral search. Shortcuts at this critical time undermine the whole purpose of renewal. Now is the opportune time to address small church issues openly and honestly.

Not unrelated to this attitude is the denominational leader's outlook toward professional movement within the system. Pastors expect to "climb the ladder," a model that clearly originates in society and is based on a reward system related to economics and status. The climbing syndrome seems simple: you pay your dues and move up the ladder. Nevertheless, it is complex, suggesting a bureaucratic rather than a companionship model.

This system of advancement is also based on the understanding that the pastor is one who has completed college and seminary at an early age. Many seminarians of the 1990s, however, bring education, training, and considerable experience from other professions, much of which can be adapted and applied to ministry. It might be hard to believe, but some pastors intentionally *choose* the supposed "entry-level" church because of their particular interests, abilities, and commitments. They believe in small church ministry! Denominational leaders must also recognize the validity and vitality of these congregations.

Statistics indicate that many who begin careers as small church pastors will continue throughout their professional ministry in the same size church. One reason is that some prefer a relational leadership style that is particularly suitable for small church ministry. Another reason is the plethora of small churches, which provides a wide field for lateral moves. This suggests application of the biblical mandate of spiritual growth as a means of strengthening the companionship model of ministry. This setting discourages bending to dominant culture norms; at the same time, it does not negate adapting to small church culture what is valuable from the dominant culture.

Because it fosters healthy esteem in the small church, the enduring pastor-people relationship model deserves careful attention. In the 1700s the call issued to a pastor was expected to be of life-long duration. Today, however, the idea of long-term commitment, which the companionship model confirms, runs counter to our culture. The companionship model offers a firm foundation from which a pastor and the people can turn problems into opportunities, together learning how to cope with the challenges of dwindling finances and a transient population.

The pastor who is committed to the companionship model must be encouraged to apply the sabbatical principle to strengthen his or her ministry by spiritual renewal and further leadership development. Learnings from sabbaticals are for the sake of the church as well as the pastor. Mutual spiritual development is a must for long-term relationships to thrive. Denominational leaders can help pastors understand the dynamics of established, enduring relationships rather than foster or encourage mobility.

It is critical for denominational leaders to develop programs that address the life and health of the small church. This not only applies to each denominational family, but also transcends denominational lines.

If it continues to be true, as Lyle Schaller has noted, that the majority of denominational leaders emerge from large churches, then those leaders working with small churches will have to acquire new skills. They need to gain experience if they are to effectively lead the small church to discover its vitality and momentum.[4] Denominational leaders unaccustomed to this environment may have to work on the development of relational skills if they are to become companions to small churches.

The Interim Minister

A key task for denominational staff is helping the congregation identify an interim minister who has the capability of relating personally in small church ministry. The interim minister's work is very important for a small church's future.

The role of the interim minister in the life of the church is shifting. Once it was thought that the role was simply to maintain ministry in the time between pastors. In response to a variety of situations many churches are seriously re-evaluating interim ministry.[5] With the encouragement of denomination staff, specific expectations are being articulated. It is not a time for "business as usual," but a time to step out in faith, to address tough issues of conflict management, economic realities, and organizational structure.

If there have been traumas, such as forced termination or loss of members, the interim may need to be extended in order to assess new realities and sensitively probe the congregation's emotions. Many formerly large churches need to adjust to life as a small church.

Interim ministries are by nature preparatory. While their function could be compared to the work of John the Baptist who prepared the way for Jesus' ministry, the interim's role is to prepare the way for new ministry in the church.

A trend today for many churches is the hiring of a retired person whose limited time commitment helps a church prepare for the employment of a bi-vocational minister. Could there be a better time than the interim to experiment with that model? It is good to test how it feels to have a pastor on location for limited hours and specific days. It is an opportune time to refine expectations, develop schedules, determine the economic package that the church can sustain, and figure out how to balance these major areas.

Other situations call for an interim minister gifted in healing to help mend broken relationships that either resulted from a pastor-people mismatch or from "power plays" among church leaders. The interim presents the framework to work together on relations and to recognize and manage conflict.

It may be a choice time to deal with structure, especially in the formerly large churches that must now reduce church boards and committees. An interim minister can assist the church because he or she can remain objective in suggesting changes that fit the new configuration of the church family.

The Seminaries

While the reality in most mainline denominations points toward shrinkage—larger churches becoming middle-sized and middle-sized contracting to smaller churches—the primary attention of the seminary appears to be focused on larger congregations.

Some students leave seminary thinking the small church is a "stepping stone" to something bigger and better. The small congregation becomes a place to gain necessary experience; once acquired—and not infrequently learned from mistakes—the pastor moves on. In some instances the testing ground is so harsh or exhausting that the individual will quit pastoral ministry altogether. Understandably a "move on after we use you" attitude erects barriers between pastors and people; in fact, this treatment is totally unacceptable. This rude manner will either prod the pastor to advance to other places of endeavor or corner the pastor into departing. Forced resignations are hurtful and painful for all involved. Many new seminary graduates have commented: "We didn't learn about the small church in seminary." They express frustration at being unprepared to deal with the dynamics unique to small churches.

Faculty role models in most seminaries tend to use "left-brain" rather than "right-brain" orientation in their teaching styles. "Left-brain" models place heavy emphasis on theory, biblical insights, and dogma, with only a light dusting of "right-brain" implications on the structure of belief evident in the life of a small church. While seminary faculty may appear to be Ph.D. academic types, some seminaries recognize the need for practical application. They augment their faculty—at least in the pastoral department—with adjunct faculty who are practitioners of ministry in a local church. How many seminaries actually encourage their students to go directly to a small church and learn firsthand all about its dynamics, and in the process actually serve and bless the congregation?

If it is true that most seminarians (regardless of age, interest, or experience) serve the small church as their first pastorate, then the impact of their seminary education is bound to influence the life of the congregations they are called to serve. New methods and programs may not be beneficial. When a seminarian imposes on the small church ministry concepts more useful in mid-range and large churches, the result will be discomfort. The best way seminaries can assist modest-size congregations is to offer courses with a deliberate focus on small church life and ministry and to use the companionship rather than the manager model of pastor-people relations.[6]

A connecting point for the seminary in addressing small church dynamics may be the Teaching Parish Program. This approach provides a natural entrance into local churches and presents ample opportunity for the pastor and the people to learn together.

While small churches tend to have a high degree of tolerance for inexperience and experimentation, their members resent being used. Integrity, trust, and sincerity are the building blocks for companionship that encourages high esteem in small churches. Seminaries must reinforce these qualities in their students.

Summary

Communities provide the context for a congregation, and it is here that small church ministry finds its greatest opportunities. But this will not just happen. The internal life of the church, including the way leadership operates and relates to the people, will influence the way a small church will respond to outside opportunities. In the process, church esteem can be impeded or enhanced. Whether you serve as pastor, interim minister, denominational staff, or as a seminary faculty member, seriously consider the companion model of leadership. It is imperative to raising small church esteem.

For Discussion and Reflection

1. What expectations does the community have of your church? Of your pastor?

2. What words, phrases, or sentences do you use when talking with your pastor or with others about your church?

3. What images best describe your church's pastor-people relationship?

4. Review the elements of the covenant your church has made with the pastor. Consider the unspoken expectations as well as the written ones.

5. How does your church work with your denomination to assure that small church needs are addressed?

6. What does your relationship with your pastor indicate about your church's esteem?

7. What words describe the feelings of your church when you are between pastors?

8. Describe the contributions interim ministers have made in the life and ministry of your church.

9. How has the seminary prepared your pastor for the work of your church?

CHAPTER V

Friction and Fighting: How Can We Stay Healthy?

Conflict is a battle. In the small church, differences of opinion concerning budgets, proposals, or methods can lead to vicious confrontations. With all this potential strife, how can we stay healthy? If conflict cannot be avoided, how can it be used? Our dominant culture's model is not very healthy, and too frequently the church adopts the methods flashed in the media.

One prevailing model is clearly seen in political campaigns. Rather than both candidates addressing their ideologies and explaining how they intend to attain their goals, they resort to crude personal attacks. When this mud slinging is practiced in the small church, things get pretty messy.

Another tactic is a demonstration of force. Modern examples include the Cuban Missile Crisis, guerrilla warfare in Central and South America, and the Persian Gulf War. It is through military prowess that missions are accomplished, be they occupying land, seizing natural resources or some profitable industry. Still another tactic is hostage taking—terrorizing and exploiting civilians as a means of obtaining a political end.

Conflicts in our world are managed by strong wills, tough policy, and cruelty. But how is conflict managed in other areas of life, particularly in church settings?

Because the small church is composed of people with unique religious journeys and faith perspectives, dissension can arise from diversity. During times of greater homogeneity in small churches there tended to be less strife. Nevertheless, the church consists of people whose feet are made of clay; all are subject to the human condition. That means conflict in the church is to be expected.

Conflict is intensified in the small church because of its lesser numbers and intimate nature. There is simply no place to conceal the fighting. In no-win situations, often the minister or some lay leader is singled out as a scapegoat. Strife always emerges when individuals cannot take personal responsibility for their own problems; conflict thrives in an atmosphere of accusation.

Despite the childhood adage "Sticks and stones will break my bones, but names will never hurt me," battles fought with words do hurt deeply. Conflicts in the church are most often fought verbally, but that does not mean these attacks are less painful or abusive than what goes on in the larger society where physical force is used in confrontations. It is painful to witness church life in the aftermath of a rift—many of the wounds never heal properly.

Conflict is accompanied by the tremendous energy that swells from aroused emotions. Sometimes these forceful expressions arise from unresolved situations from a person's, or in some instances from a church's, past. The challenge is to turn highly charged negative energy to positive expressions.

Conflict in the small church is like a thunder and lightning storm. Sometimes a heavy front blows through quickly and then calm is restored just as swiftly; other times a storm buffets and destroys everything in its wake. Once lightning rods were used as grounds to channel electricity away from where the force could do the most harm.

All too often in the small church, the pastor becomes the congregation's lightning rod—the people hope their leader can withstand all the verbal bolts and still maintain a clear head to redirect the surges in positive ways. We keep learning that pastors are very human and often do not have any more ability than the church members to withstand relentless attempts to discredit individual worth and undermine ministry activities.

The church is called to affirm rather than to attack. Yes, anger can produce tremendous negative energy; affirmation, on the other hand, generates enormous positive energy for ministry. Yet someone has suggested that it takes twenty positive statements to overcome a negative one. If this is true, then sympathize with the pastor of a small church who must locate and tap enough positive force to maintain an effective ministry. It will not be easy.

In some instances the pastor becomes the victim of conflict, and in the process is made so uncomfortable that his or her only recourse is to evacuate before the conflict escalates to the next level. The church is bound to suffer when the pastor-people relationship terminates in a storm of human emotions.

If the pastor has not been able to relocate and the conflict remains unresolved, or if the conflict erupts into an open battle, the pastor may be forced to negotiate a termination date and agree to a cash settlement. In response to the increasing number of *forced* terminations, many denominations have developed guidelines to assist churches in creating fair compensation when issues cannot be resolved.

In the United States the church's moral influence on community life seems diminished. Churches were once perceived as centers of integrity whose leadership was respected and valued. Today, the church tends to turn inward, concentrating all its energies on its own internal workings. This creates a dilemma because the church must live in the world.

The church is called to live a vibrant life in the midst of cultural pressures; in fact, its very way of seeing and being may run counter to the dominant culture. Instead of using the world's means to resolve conflict—models learned in the workplace, borrowed from the military, gleaned from videos, or copied from the government—the church's distinction is to practice those models that grow out of a relationship with Jesus Christ and the church's biblical roots.

Our experience suggests an alarming increase in the number of pastors who are the victims in unresolved church conflicts[1]. When a pastor loses his or her leadership role in the process of helping a church face its internal problems, this may only be symptomatic of a deeper cause. The fault might not be centered in the pastor's personality or leadership style. Instead, the real issue might be the church's inability to relate to or accept any pastoral authority. In any event, conflicts that are not faced and worked through will only explode when and where a church and its clergy least expect it.

When conflict remains suppressed and the pastor is not directly confronted, church members may decide to depart. They may express their dissatisfaction by attending elsewhere or by withholding finances from the church. If money is power, then lost revenue may force the pastor or church to change behavior patterns. However, this change will not occur automatically. The underlying issues must be addressed openly. Communication is the *key* to change.

We usually notice a conflict's *symptoms* and miss the root cause. Cutting through the layers of unresolved problems is similar to peeling an onion: To reach the core demands time, energy, and perseverance while tears burn in the eyes. The process may be excruciating, but the painful paring must be done if the church is to reach the center of the conflict. Even if the incision hurts, the truth does set one free.

In *Leading Your Church Through Conflict*, Speed Leas identifies five levels of conflict: *Level I* Problems to Solve, where the purpose is to fix the problem; *Level II* Disagreement, where broken trust leads to insecurity and factionalism; *Level III* Contest, where the win-lose dynamic is in effect and each faction seeks victory; *Level IV* Fight/Flight, where hostility simmers, boiling into attack and counter-attack; *Level V* Intractable Situations, where the no-win dynamic is in effect, and the situation spirals out of control.[2] Leas' naming of these stages helps those of us who regularly deal with conflict formulate strategies appropriate to the conflict level.

In our work we continue to peel away the onion skin to move the small church toward behavior patterns that are proactive rather than reactive. The decision to address conflict can be the first step on the road to high church esteem.

In *Each Teach Two*, Donald DeMott uses Richard Beale's creative process in which the *initiating conflict* is presented with its thesis and antithesis; the second phase is the *preparation period* where data are gathered and presented; the third is the *incubation stage*, an unconscious process that progresses toward the *insight stage* where patterns begin to emerge. It is at the *work phase* where agreements can be made, leading to the final step of *synthesis*. Using Beale's system should lead to a win-win conclusion.[3] However, our experience suggests that most small churches have not yet implemented this productive means of resolving conflict.

A more realistic picture suggests that friction between a church and its pastor tends to follow the levels described in Leas' *Leadership and Conflict*. They advance from the initial conflict to attack or they withdraw.[4] This pattern seems especially true in low-esteem churches, where it is more difficult to negotiate agreements and resolve contentious issues.

Anthony Pappas, in *Entering the World of the Small Church*, encourages people in small churches to heed even the *feelings* of dissonance. He maintains there is usually something substantive that generates these feelings.[5] Finding and defining the issue can spur responsible persons toward an analysis that leads to identifying—and ultimately choosing—possible strategies. The choice then becomes the basis for setting objectives, and the implementation plan leads to the resolution of the issues and the stabilization of situations. At last a church can move forward to achieve and maintain high esteem.

Unsettled and unmediated problems producing friction in the small church can harm the life and ministry of a church for many years. We are committed to helping churches alter their behavior patterns, so they can address conflict rather than remain at variance.

Edwin Friedman, using the family systems approach outlined in *Generation to Generation*, suggests conflict arises when something is out of balance in the family system. Problems occur because of circumstances beyond anyone's control but which, nevertheless, touch and affect the life of the church. He further proposes that to regain control someone will have to initiate transforming the negative, habitual behavior patterns. A person must be intentional about squarely facing the causes precipitating the strife. A church member has to be willing to say: "We're not going to do business this way any more." Determination and courage to implement change may not be enough. While a laudable sentiment, this type of proclamation often frustrates those trying to change; admitting defeat, people resettle into former patterns. Friedman introduces concepts related to *third-party intervention*—namely, *coaching* and *non-anxious presence*. The third party assists in maintaining open channels of communication. Friedman notes that friction is frequently symptomatic of an underlying dynamic, and unless that particular dynamic is confronted conflicts will continue to flare up in some other arenas in the church's life.[6]

An alternate approach to conflict is to use the Twelve Step Program[7], a system in which people take responsibility for their own behavior patterns. The basics of this approach may be summed up as follows:

1. Quit the "blame game;"
2. Apologize and if necessary make restitution to those who have been harmed;
3. Get one's life right with the Creator; and
4. Begin living responsibly.

Applied to the small church and using the church's theological terms, it could translate this way:

1. Quit making scapegoats out of leaders;
2. Reject embedded patterns of decision making and repent;
3. Accept God's forgiveness;
4. Become intentional about the life of the church; and
5. Go forward to do God's work in the world.

Many in our society are familiar with the Twelve Step program as it applies to the various anonymous groups organized to help alcoholics, gamblers, overeaters, and the narcotics-dependent. Here is a possible adaptation of the Twelve Step program for small churches in resolving conflict:

1. Admit that your small church has a conflict that is out of control.
2. Believe that God can use conflict creatively.
3. Decide to turn the conflict over to God's care, but also seek outside assistance (e.g., mediation centers, The Alban Institute, denominational staff persons).
4. With their assistance, search for the basis of the conflict, keeping in mind the need to understand root causes, not merely the outward symptoms.
5. Create worship or small group events by which you may repent of any sins of omission or commission that may have contributed to the conflict.
6. Prepare for God's removal of any barriers to resolution by being open to new ways of handling church issues.
7. Seek God's forgiveness in this situation to assure letting go of the conflict.
8. Identify persons hurt through the conflict situation.
9. Plan and prepare ways to make amends with persons hurt in the conflict. A mediator may be needed to assist the process.
10. Continue to pay attention to the dynamics that led to the uncon trollable conflict. (While this pattern is needed in all situations, it is absolutely essential in those situations that lead to polarization with pastors and frequently end in forced terminations.)
11. Develop the church's spiritual life through worship, prayer, education, and mission involvement.

12. Share the message of reconciliation with other churches in your denomination and community. This pattern is helpful in assisting other churches to develop the confidence needed to understand conflict as the "birth pangs of a new age."

While there is a pattern of anonymity in the addictive-anonymous programs, accountability is also built in as part of the process. So in addition to owning one's behavior patterns there has to be a willingness to help others by sharing one's own story, and by taking the initiative in working with those who reach out for help. This modification of the Twelve Step approach is simply another way of addressing conflict as a church moves toward higher esteem.

Whatever approach a church decides to use to address its conflict, *ground rules* need to be established. A helpful set comes from Keith Huttenlocker:[8]

It is okay to—

Confront
For example: "I find it difficult when you . . ."

Contend
To set forth one's opinion clearly

Disagree
For example: "I see it rather differently from that."

Accentuate
For example: "This is a major concern to me."

Indicate
For example: "I can live with (this), but not with (that)."

Express concern
To state facts that document the existence of a problem

Request
For example: "May I ask that in the future you . . ."

Confess injury
Relate an event or remarks that caused pain.

It is *not* okay to:

Condemn
For example: "You have absolutely no business . . ."

Contrive
To line up political support for one's position

Discredit
For example: "This is a stupid idea that will never work."

Exaggerate
For example: "This is the worst I can imagine."

Dictate
For example: "You either (this) or I will (that)."

Place blame
To make generalizations that implicitly or explicitly indict
another

Demand
For example: "I'm telling you that from now on you had
better . . ."

Inflict guilt
Induce shame on another for his or her conduct or words

In addressing conflict, the small church is also faced with theological and sociological diversity. In *Frameworks: Patterns for Living and Believing Today*, Douglas Walrath pushes us to understand this diversity so that we might minister effectively in these times.[9] Every one of us operates according to our own framework from which we understand the world and try to live in it. However, that often makes us egocentric, believing our own values and ways are the normative, "correct" ways.

One approach to treating diversity with its potential for conflict and subsequent lowered esteem is to create *covenant prayer groups*.[10] This model is designed to incorporate diversity in the small groups that join for prayer. To strengthen a church's ability to cope when all other avenues have failed, prayer may be the only resort to resolve differences and allow reconnection with the community of faith in its divine purpose. Covenant prayer groups can renew and stabilize church esteem.

Summary

As long as we are human, conflict is here to stay. It can be a healthy means of stimulating the church to move forward in response to God's ever new call to ministry. Friction and fighting can be avoided, managed, or resolved; circumstances will dictate which approach will work better.

Several approaches to conflict management are offered, however, the church and the people involved must jointly choose which one best fits the situation. There are tools; there are mediators; there are conflict managers. The urgent need is for resolution. Let God supply your small church with the courage needed to recognize and admit the friction and fighting; pray for the willingness to respond and the wisdom to work through to a solution.

For Reflection and Discussion

1. What are the implications of conflict in the life of your church? What opportunities do friction and fighting provide for helping the church regain or reclaim its church esteem?

2. Use the story at Mizpah (Genesis 31:44-53) as a symbol of what is needed to create patterns for addressing and resolving conflict—i.e., creating a safe environment, a place of trust, invoking God's presence in helping persons keep their side of the covenant.

3. Name the uneasy feelings that make you think that there is something amiss in your church.

4. Identify several ways in which you can deal with the uneasy feelings within the church's life.

5. Identify the resources available to your church for addressing the issue of conflict in church life.

CHAPTER VI

On the Road to High Esteem

We have so far defined what a small church is, and we have identified esteem as an important but complex identity issue. We have also looked at both a high and a low esteem church, listened to the *feelings* expressed by participants in a small church that successfully made the transition to high esteem, and considered some of the factors affecting these churches. We delved into the dynamics of small churches, examining the difference size makes. Now it is time to study further some real-life churches on the road to high esteem.

Hillview Community Baptist Church

Out of the denomination's thrust to establish new churches the Hillview Community Baptist Church was born. The record indicates it was a breech birth. The individuals who formed the new church brought with them varied experiences. Some were high spirited, seeing this as an adventure. Others came from a church where theological differences impaired their ability to work well together.

Understandably, those from a fragmented church sought a place of refuge. Even though the individuals who emerged from a church split seemed energetic, the negative source of their energy affected their focus. They still needed to confront the anger from past experiences. In contrast, church planters coming from more stable situations have unencumbered and focused energy and are ready to pursue new challenges with vigor and vitality. In reviewing its history, the church finally began to understand how these backgrounds and personal factors affected the church's journey in its infant stage.

Through the years the church had been involved in several studies with little or no follow-up, but when the timing seemed right, the people decided to take control of the church's destiny.

Conflict with the pastor became the catalyst for the church body to initiate changes. In the midst of the ensuing turmoil, the church invited Dr. Steve Burt, then a New England small church consultant, to immerse the church in an intensive weekend assessment project. In the process the church identified its assets and strengths and noted its liabilities; issues were articulated and conflicts were recognized. Dr. Burt followed the consultation with a detailed written report that offered recommendations for the church to consider. Topping those suggestions was the call for reconciliation between the two divergent groups responsible for organizing the new church. Two individuals represented the factions.

After the pastor's termination, the church experienced a lengthy period of pulpit-supply preachers until the church was able to locate an interim person. He served for three months, and the continuity refreshed the weary congregation. He listened to the people, allowing them a chance to rid themselves of accumulated negative feelings. It was a rewarding time of spiritual healing and development.

The next interim also served the church for three months. She dedicated herself to helping the church establish solid foundations, beginning that process by prompting the church to consider its formative years. How did she do it?

She combined preaching themes and thematic Bible studies. One effective method she used was to first focus on the individual and then gradually move to the church's corporate life. Here is a sample of her pattern of reflection: (1) Examine your feelings about being in the wilderness and describe how you cope there. (2) What resources did Jesus use in his wilderness situations? In what ways was this preparatory for the commencement of his ministry? (3) How does your study of this event relate to your experiences in your church? Using the passages of Exodus 3:7-4:17; Matthew 4:1-17; Luke 1:26-55; and Acts 1:15-26, she addressed the topic of "Beginnings."

Next the interim minister, considering the Family Systems approach outlined by Rabbi Edwin Friedman,[1] led the Hillview church family through another series of Bible studies (Matthew 1:18-25; Mark 3:31-36; Mark 6:1-6; John 2:1-12; John 19:25-27). Through these passages she lovingly challenged the participants to face anger, family fighting, cclebrations, time conflicts, interest and expectations, and religious values. In this way the people began to grasp the elements that each contributed when they first began the church. They were able to check all the unarticulated assumptions inherent in the charter members and the early additions to the church.

A study based on Mark 14:3-9 helped the people connect the role of sacrificial faithfulness to the life of the church. Abundant examples were found in Scripture: The bonding of Ruth and Naomi (Ruth 1:1-22); Jesus in Gethsemane (Mark 14:32-42); the restoration of life to a girl and life to a woman (Luke 8:40-56); the dishonest manager (Luke 16:10-13); the widow and the unjust judge (Luke 18:1-9); and the widow's offering, and the destruction of the temple foretold (Luke 21:1-14). Again the pattern was followed: working with the individual before progressing to the corporate.

The interim pastor's next theme was "Confronting Conflict." When speaking about friction and anger, she included the fears that often accompany these feelings. As biblical grounds, she used these texts: Jesus cursing the fig tree and cleansing the temple (Mark 11:11-15); the betrayal and arrest of Jesus (Luke 22:47-53); and rules for new life (Ephesians 4:25-27).

Based on the parable of the talents (Matthew 25:14-30), the church considered the concept of the steady servant. Through this teaching, the interim pastor helped individuals identify their own gifts and determine ways to use them. Wisely she also prepared the church for her departure, which would coincide with the anniversary of the loss of their permanent pastor. She focused on assisting the church to order its priorities for the remainder of their time together.

The Easter Sunday topic, "A Second Look," centered on the resurrection of Jesus (John 20:1-18). Through this reflection she encouraged individuals to examine their own experiences and make "tomb" and "resurrection" associations. In a similar vein, another theme for contemplation was "Choose Life." Here the object was to become connected with life-giving rather than life- denying activities.

As the church family examined its roots, they realized that the present facilities were not designed in accordance with their original proposal. What caused the glitch? People felt unsettled in their inability to trace what went wrong in the planning and construction stage. However, in working through Hillview's beginnings, the church finally accepted the building as is, even though the present design did not reflect their original intention. From that point they were able to start alterations, creating a more hospitable, attractive, and utilitarian facility.

Under the extended leadership of an interim minister, the church began to address what consultant Steve Burt recommended. The most visible are the physical changes to the building. The church now uses the front rather than the side entrance; a parking lot now services the front door; a wall has been removed inside the building to make easier passage for the people and provide access to beverages during fellowship time; new carpeting awaits installation; and the church sign attracts attention. These physical renovations symbolize the church moving from low to high esteem.

Because it has decided to intentionally face the issues of its corporate life, the church has grown, learning healthier ways of dealing with internal conflict.

With the help of interim ministry this church has been able to venture beyond a past that no one completely understood. A recent visit to the church revealed positive attitudes and a lighter, brighter atmosphere.

Analysis

What factors can be identified in this case study?

1. Organizational Development. It appears that Hillview's organizational development got stuck in its formative phase. The cultural climate of the sixties did not lend itself to understanding dynamics that brought together two divergent church groups into a new organizational structure. Any negative elements were simply swept under the carpet.

2. Decision Making. It appears that something went awry in the transmission of the church's decision regarding the blueprint design of its building. Not wanting errors of this magnitude to happen again, the church has moved toward decision making by consensus.

3. Conflict. Conflict is like an abscess: Left untreated, it infects the entire body. In this instance, strife occurred in the pastor-people relationship, which led to the departure of the pastor. A positive response to this was the church's resolve to tackle its identity issues and examine its behavior patterns.

4. Communication. Communication deteriorated within the church family. Meetings degenerated into marathon sessions Some with injured feelings left the church family. The congregation committed itself to creating better systems of communication that would include rather than exclude people.

Strategies

1. Organizational Development. This foundational issue was addressed by the interim minister in Bible studies geared to help the church come to terms with its beginnings. Members began to recognize how unspoken assumptions obstructed the flow of church life.

2. Decision Making. The church tried out the consensus model for making decisions. While the process is slower than the majority rule of *Robert's Rules of Order*, it is most adaptable to small church settings because everyone has a voice, and everyone "owns" the final decision.

3. Conflict. Using the biblical model of facing the person with whom the conflict exists, and with the help of a skilled interim minister, issues causing contention were mediated and relationships were reconciled.

4. Communication. Through the participatory Bible study model of reflection and sharing, participants enhanced their communication skills.

For Discussion and Reflection

1. What are the issues keeping your church from being on the road to high esteem?

2. How can your church address issues? How can your church transform these issues from *blocks* to *benefits*?

3. Who is needed to help your church go forward on the road to high esteem?

4. How do your organizational patterns affect the church's esteem?

5. How are decisions made in your church? Are persons enfranchised or disenfranchised?

6. How do you address conflict in your church?

7. Describe the various communication patterns in your church.

United Methodist Church, White River Junction, Vermont

Unlike Hillview Community Baptist, which has remained fairly level in its membership since its inception, White River Methodist was a typical "formerly big" church. In 1961, this downtown "tall steeple church" peaked at nearly 800 members. It was a unique and awkward pastoral "charge" because its solo pastor had to serve White River *and* a smaller Family church (90 members, 30-35 at worship) in North Hartland five miles down the road.

In 1983 the worship attendance at White River Methodist was 25-40; the long neglected membership rolls listed 468 members. The downtown site showed twenty years of deferred maintenance. A plus was the acquisition of a modern parsonage in a pleasant residential neighborhood more than a mile from the church. It had been hastily purchased because the previous pastor had been terrorized by residents of a low-income housing project near the former parsonage.

The church was broke and deeply in debt; for instance, a substantial past-due winter fuel bill still could not be paid in July. There were no Sunday morning church school classes for children or adults, no active men's or women's groups, no building usage by outside groups (except rental of two rooms to house a kindergarten whose rent barely covered the utilities). There were no fund-raising activities. The budget called for $38,000; pledges totaled $15,000. The church was three years behind on its financial obligations to the denomination. And no one wanted to serve on any committee. After two exhausting and disenchanting years, the young pastor packed up and left. That was mid 1983.

In 1987 White River Methodist entered its fifth and final year with the pastor who reorganized it. Worship attendance averaged 70-90; four years of gleaning and purging the membership rolls brought the membership total to 242. A licensed lay pastor was hired part time to assist; together both pastors only served White River Methodist. (The 40-year "yoked" parish relationship dissolved in 1986—the Family church in North Hartland finally got its own part-time pastor).

Not only had the overdue fuel bill been retired, but new efficient furnaces had been installed in the two downtown buildings and in the parsonage. Fresh paint and improved lighting could be seen throughout the facility, topped with new roofing. An efficient 10-burner gas stove graced the church kitchen, and a passenger elevator had been installed. Even a new steeple would be provided later in the year. The denominational askings and benevolences were paid in full, and the increased budget of $54,000 had almost $35,000 pledged toward it.

The church became innovative in its planning and quickly gained momentum. Members now operated "Second Hand Rose"—a used clothing ministry open two afternoons a week; they housed a special-needs preschool called Learning to Listen (the Kindergarten had left in 1983 when Vermont mandated public kindergartens); and they provided space for a new social service umbrella group called The Family Place. Alcoholics Anonymous, Parents Without Partners, Boy Scouts, Adult Children of Alcoholics, and various groups met at the church weekly or monthly. The church housed the Community Dinners Program, a soup kitchen that fed 20-60 people two nights a week, the program being staffed ecumenically by eight rotating teams representing area churches. Two elementary church school classes and a lay-led adult class met Sunday mornings. As many as five different lay-led Bible studies were in progress during the week. A prayer study group, a family issues film series, and several Scott Peck study groups met at different times over a span of four years.

Special worship and ecumenical services, including a predominantly laity-preached Good Friday Service based on the seven last words of Christ from the cross, were well attended throughout the year. Seven of the church's lay members formed the core of the Eastern Vermont Ecumenical Lay Preaching Group (EVELPG), which provided regular and occasional pulpit supply for rural small churches (some without pastors, some with pastors needing vacation coverage). The EVELPG recruited, trained, and coordinated the assignments of lay preachers. Eventually this group expanded to fifteen persons who represented seven denominations and served as many as twenty-five churches.[2]

Many of the church's members previously inactive on boards of nonprofit organizations or para-church organizations began to volunteer, serving groups such as Parents Without Partners, Learning to Listen, The Family Place, Hospice, and an emergency shelter known as The Haven. Church members helped organize and staff the ecumenical Good Friday Hunger Walk, the annual CROP Hunger Walk, and other charity events. White River provided a Community Dinners team, relocated a Cambodian family, and contributed financially to the relocation of several other refugees. A group of recent retirees volunteered at Dartmouth-Hitchcock Hospital, and another group began serving tea and offering companionship once a week at a local nursing home. Several women formed a quartet and sang regularly at the same nursing home.

When the time came to consider what the church's needs might be for a successor to the departing pastor, the church's Administrative Council engaged in medium-range planning. They studied the goals and direction of the church and its ministries, and then considered how the pastor might best participate. The Pastor-Parish Relations Committee trained its members intensively in the art of interviewing for a pastor. Borrowing an idea from their congregational Search Committee counterparts in the free church system, White River did something relatively unheard of for a United Methodist Church. They took the initiative and collected historical and program data about the church; next they added a church pictorial directory; and third, they amassed a hefty packet of literature from the community, hospitals, schools, recreational facilities, and social service agencies.

They went a step further in their thorough effort to introduce potential candidates to their area and congregation. They videotaped their local area (the Upper Valley) and their town (White River Junction) with its schools and colleges and its social and recreational services. They included church functions and activities—worship, a fund-raising turkey supper, a Community Dinners team at work, and lots of members stating what the church meant to them. Finally, the departing pastor spoke for five minutes addressing what he considered to be the church's primary issues and future prospects. Very early in the process, the packet of materials and the videotape were forwarded to the District Superintendent; he in turn made these materials available to potential candidates. Thus a useful presorting process was set in motion.

Analysis

What made the difference at White River Methodist? What made them turn things around after so many years of decline and despair? There were a number of factors that can be identified.

1. Tenure
The clergy person stated clearly in the interview and restated periodically

that he would partner with the church for five years. From the outset the congregation felt secure and did not have to worry about losing this key leader. Establishing a time frame meant they could initiate plans and make steady progress in their projects.

2. Denominational support

The District Superintendent assured the congregation that their pastor, barring any truly extraordinary circumstances, would be available to them for the five years. The church later petitioned their Conference for a "jubilee," requesting to be absolved of several years' worth of unpaid denominational obligations. The denomination, which they felt had turned adversarial in recent years, surprised them with an agreement to wipe the slate clean. Later the Conference assisted White River with low-cost loans to catch up on some of the deferred maintenance items; in addition, an arm of the denomination granted seed money for the church's handicapped access project.

3. Clergy leadership

The incoming pastor knew something about demographics, church decline, and organizational dynamics. He loved and thoroughly understood the dynamics of small churches, including the distinctive needs of the "formerly big" church. Most important, he related well to people. He fathomed coalition building from the inside of an organization, and was comfortable and accustomed to the workings of outside groups like social service agencies. He believed strongly in empowering the laity for ministry and in turning them loose, even if it meant risking failure. This pastor knew what it meant to lead a small, *relational* organization and the importance of his role as *vision-bearer*. He was deft in the usage of visuals (newsletters, bulletins, press releases, bulletin boards, etc.) to create *feedback loops* that affirmed the congregation. The pastor had a good working knowledge of *conflict management*, and he guided the people to deal with problems out in the open. He taught them that conflict could be considered an opportunity for growth rather than a harmful experience to avoid. Last, he operated according to the pastor *companion model* and was not reluctant to express *appreciation and love* for the congregation.

4. Identity

The pastor helped the church realize that while it was no longer a large church, there was exciting, tremendous potential for esteem in *claiming its identity as a small church.*

5. Structure and organization for action

There was a lot of work to do. The unwieldy board structure had to be abandoned. It was a tandem, comprised of a large Administrative Board with its own set of subcommittees and a large Council on Ministries with its separate subcommittees. In its place, they favored one single-cell board consisting of twenty-three people sitting on an Administrative Council. Though slightly cumbersome, it certainly was an operational improvement. The new Council convened on a monthly basis for an hour and a half, gathering around a large group of tables so people could face each other. Many of the denomination's prescribed offices were allowed to remain vacant; instead, people channeled their energies into *action and task committees.* People valued each other's views, and respected one another's freedoms to accomplish their designated tasks without interference. Completed tasks were appreciated and publicized. The committees and groups achieved an inner and outward balance: Some involved themselves diligently with the church's institutional maintenance issues; others assumed a posture not seen in decades: *outreaching.*[3]

6. Coalition-building

The pastor saw that the church could best identify needs and engage in local mission by *a partnership* with area social service agencies and para-church organizations. The first half-hour of each monthly Administrative Council meeting was set aside for educating the Council; a guest (social or community action worker or agency director) was invited to give a brief presentation and answer questions about his or her particular mission, agency, or charity. Within a short time many church members were serving on the boards of nonprofit agencies.

7. Re-establishing biblical literacy and small groups

The pastor convinced the Council that the number of study groups the church could support did not need to be limited by his time. Lay persons could study the Bible in small groups without having an authority figure presiding. The church invested in inductive Bible study guides and used a small group model that called for weekly rotation of leadership among group members. All these studies were conducted with laity empowered as leaders, with the pastor only visiting each group on occasion.[4] This freed him for other programs and for community coalition work. The original five Bible study groups multiplied; now the participants became the leaders of new small group programs, using the Dobson film discussion series, several Scott Peck study groups, and a prayer study group.[5]

8. Fund-raising projects
From the 1940s through the 1960s the church sponsored a turkey supper open to the public. One pastor shamed and bullied the congregation into discontinuing the dinners; in the process, he eliminated a main source for funding the budget—and his salary. At the same time, he damaged the church's esteem. The re-organizing pastor *listened* to people, not only empathizing with their pain, but wisely recognizing that people's ability to work together and successfully earn money was integral to their esteem. As a result, he encouraged them to re-establish the supper program they enjoyed doing. Besides, it bolstered a positive identity in the larger community. ("Now here's a delicious turkey supper served by a friendly church whose dedicated people work together!") The idea succeeded, partly because it tapped into a strong affirming behavior.[6] People with the know-how rolled up their sleeves and made the program a success. The paid turkey suppers stabilized the budget as well as the church's rickety sense of self-worth.[7]

9. Finances
A multi-faceted approach to finances was used. The fundraisers contributed and their results were publicized and celebrated. Coalition-building efforts paid off. When the kindergarten moved out, a pre-school moved in, paying a more realistic rent. A used-clothing ministry was launched, using part of the empty educational building; volunteers were mobilized, providing a ministry streamlined to the church's purposes that also netted about $3,000 of income per year. Loans were obtained from the Conference to undertake work projects on deferred maintenance. The furnaces, roof, insulation, and storm windows paid for themselves in utilities savings. As the esteem level went up, the pledging went up; as the pledging went up, the budgeted benevolences went up. Stewardship became serious business.

10. Work force and volunteers
Rather than complain about the average age of the congregation, the

church began to garner the retired folks' experience and take advantage of their willingness and availability. Rather than match a job with someone to do it, people were encouraged to consider their time and talents, and to choose work that would be meaningful to them. Of course, many did the menial tasks that needed to be done, but still there was a different attitude. People felt they had a say in the volunteer work. They no longer felt coerced into working for the church—they could exercise choice, and their labors were regularly acknowledged.

11. Luck, grace, or maybe a bit of both
A cluster of high energy people retired from their jobs during the second, third, and fourth year and were excited about the new life in the church. The lay-led Bible studies and small groups helped them feel comfortable in assuming other leadership roles. They now also felt they had a working knowledge of the Bible, the lack of which had held many of them back for years, though they had been too embarrassed to admit it. Studying Mark's Gospel provided them with something precious: a common language and a new shared frame of reference.

12. Small victories first
First things first: Tackle the overdue heating bill. The new pastor immediately used the debt as a rallying point. After a worship service, he symbolically burned the paid invoice in a public ceremony.

13. Stewardship of the buildings
The under-used buildings had been seen as a *liability* for years, but the Council began looking at them as *assets*. A free hospital bed, which had been advertised in the newspaper, was picked up and stored in the education building. The next church bulletin and newsletter carried a notice that it was available free on loan to anyone in the community, an offer not limited to church membership. Within two weeks someone borrowed it! And that was only the beginning. The newly reorganized women's group purchased a used wheelchair for $50; from all over town they began amassing canes, crutches, walkers, toilet seat extenders, and shower seats. Another hospital bed was donated. This is how the church's Hospital Equipment Loan Program started. Members joyfully volunteered their time in delivering some of the items to housebound persons.

The church became so active itself and so busy accommodating outside groups such as Alcoholics Anonymous and Parents Without Partners that scheduling became a critical issue. Now the congregation had to carefully tend to stewardship of time and space. But what a blessing to endure after so many years of an empty house!

14. "Cheap thrills" programming
The church stopped trying to be a Program Church and came up with less ambitious and less energy-taxing projects that could raise esteem. Through a variety of size- and context-appropriate ideas, the church had fun, gained high visibility, and expended minimal effort and resources. (See the chapter on Programmatic Approach.)[8]

15. Consensus decision making
The Council switched from majority rule to a consensus model of decision making. (Any one person can block consensus by objecting, however, decisions are passed by everyone either saying "yes" or by agreeing *not to say "no"*.) At first it was a difficult process to incorporate, but it ensured that every voice would be seriously regarded. After all, anyone could prevent consensus by one vote. The model shaped a tremendously strong and unified group.

16. Sensible Transformations to Worship
The *structure* of the worship service was modified to emphasize that everyone should feel part of a small church "where everybody knows your name." The congregation agreed to wear *name tags* for the sake of making newcomers feel comfortable in their assimilation. A blurb in the bulletin explained the *rationale*.

White River also *thought* about their theology of worship and elected to sacrifice a quiet worship atmosphere. Someone had said it was "somber and depressed, reflecting the church's identity." They instituted a time of greeting midpoint in the service when everyone was invited to take a full five minutes, walk around, clear their heads of cobwebs, introduce themselves, rejoice in each other's presence, or even to arrange meeting times. One person compared it favorably to a welcome "commercial break." Deciding to innovate was not easy for the Council because changes—and the intentions behind these modifications—might be misconstrued. Some might even criticize that the service was not "religious enough." For the first time, however, the Council wondered *whom exactly they were trying to please* as well as question the purpose behind the innovation. They experimented with the break and liked it so much they described it as a "wonderful, warm free-for-all."

The *printed order of service* was shortened from two pages to one by not printing the litanies. Instead, highly relevant *homemade litanies* (e.g., newspaper headline litanies) were developed and used.[9] Bulletins with blank back covers were purchased, leaving the third and fourth pages open for activities and people announcements and thus creating a sense of life and spontaneity. Bulletins were also redesigned to be *user friendly* to the unchurched, giving page numbers for such (assumed) standards as the Lord's Prayer and the Doxology; no abbreviations (UMW, PPRC, CWS, etc.) were used unless the actual full name had been given somewhere else in the bulletin.[10] *Pew Bibles* were purchased, and together the congregation read aloud the Gospel selection for the day.

Lay persons were not only encouraged to preach, they were *trained* how to research, write, and deliver a sermon.

Special food collection drives and special item offerings provided opportunities for creativity in the worship service. The church took advantage of the power of *visual impact* on newcomers and, as a way of reinforcing their own good actions, they asked people to carry these select items to the altar during the singing of the first hymn.[11]

17. Innovation

The pastor and later the Council encouraged the introduction of new concepts and gave latitude even for failure. Ideas that worked were celebrated, publicized within the church and community, and often written up in denomination or national publications. Some brainstorms that worked effectively include the following: a pre-marital banquet for engaged couples;[12] a World Communion Bread Fest, using homemade breads and toppings;[13] Shopping Bag Sundays to stock the local emergency food pantry;[14] a Rural Life Days celebration and Cow Flop Drop fundraiser; and creation of a video and packet as part of the search process for the next pastor.

18. Setting priorities and clarifying expectations

The Council and pastor were very open about the use of the pastor's time. He presented them with three detailed *time studies* in the first two years and led them through an exercise that revealed the wide range and impossible number of *expectations* that people assumed he would fulfill.[15] From this exercise, they put in order a few priorities. By noting the pastor's time constraints and admitting that some expectations were just plain ridiculous, the Council carried its own weight and freed the pastor's time for his work with re-organization and new growth. (For example, visiting members who were housebound did not rank as high a priority as did the development of newcomer programs. This was a hard choice to make, but that was the Council and pastor's option.)

19. Articulating the vision

The pastor—in worship, in sermons, in newsletters and bulletins, in Council and committee meetings, in conversations with individuals— constantly articulated, restated, reshaped, and painted pictures of *the vision*. But he did not stand alone. As the small groups flourished, and as the new single-cell Council came together through consensus decision making, everyone else began envisioning the new self-image of "the small church with the big heart." An inspiring sense of purpose emerged: to feed the hungry, clothe the naked, shelter the homeless, welcome the stranger. This was certainly more edifying than the old road they had taken: combatting the issues of institutional survival. People began to feel like they were part of a *church* again, a *community of faith acting together to do the work of Christ*. This small church now clarified, articulated, and *claimed* its identity and gained its self-esteem.

20. A Symbol and a Rallying Point

The Council researched the value of symbols and deliberately chose to replace the church's steeple as a significant rallying point. After a storm in 1963, the damaged steeple had been removed and was never replaced. Ironically, its removal marked the beginning of the church's decline. The rejuvenated congregation wanted to restore the steeple to symbolize its return to wholeness as a church. Just before the Christmas of 1988— twenty-five years after the original rotting steeple was hauled away—a construction crane lowered the new steeple onto the roof of White River Junction United Methodist Church.

For Discussion and Reflection

1. What is your church's identity as expressed by insiders? By newcomers? By people in the community? By neighboring churches? By the denomination?

2. What identity does the worship service reflect to insiders? To newcomers?

3. What do your printed materials communicate? Overtly? Subconsciously?

4. Are you an open or a closed congregation? Are you like French bread, warm and tasty on the inside, but hard to break into from the outside?

5. Are your people enfranchised? Does everyone not only *get a chance* to express himself or herself, but do they actually *do it*?

6. Are you frightened by the idea of consensus decision making? Could you allow one person to block you from doing something if he or she felt that strongly against it? What would happen to your sense of group, initially as well as over the long haul?

7. How do you use your space? For insiders? For outsiders? A combination? How can you see assets where before you had seen liabilities?

8. Do you seriously guard, respect, and not monopolize your pastor's time? How can you better understand it? What hard choices do you need to make about priorities?

9. How do you fund-raise? Are there other methods that might be fun, esteem-raising, and suitable for your folks in their particular context?

10. How well does your governing structure work for you? Is it designed for inward focus, institutional maintenance, and service to the church, or is it designed for outward focus and service to the world?

11. Is your church an equipping station where saints are prepared for ministry? How can you improve in this area?

12. What are your most innovative programs and ideas? How can you develop and implement more?

13. Do you allow failure, or as a church do you refrain from taking risks?

14. How do you see conflict? As something to avoid or as an opportunity for growth and progress?

15. How can you raise morale and esteem in your church?

CHAPTER VII

Let's Take the High Road

My hunch is that raising the esteem of small churches will top our agenda for the next few decades. Why? A host of pressures will continue to mount, including inflation, membership decline, the graying of North America, continuing social change, wholesale population shifts, a general climate more favorable to large than to small, denominational stroking, funding allocated to church-growth projects, and other issues we covered in the preceding chapters. However, if we can raise a small church's esteem, we can also raise its sights.

Low esteem is not an issue by itself; it is not a single ailment with a single cure. There is a multitude of causes and factors. Let's look at a few, keeping in mind that in real church situations the causes are not as easily isolated as they are here for our examination.

In institutions, low esteem that stems from a *single cause* is usually but not always temporary. One parish I worked with was driven to its knees trying to please the pastor. The congregation felt that nothing they did was ever good enough. The people complained, "He was always telling us—from the pulpit, no less—that we were too small, too poor, too selfish, too lacking in commitment. Thank God he left. Thank God!" The next pastor was very loving and affirming, and the church began to thrive. For the most part, the low esteem persisted as long as the pastor's unprofitable service.

Multiple factors can pummel esteem. Often a complex problem is mistakenly perceived as having a single cause. One example is the outdated or deteriorating facility, such as the 1950s white elephant the present congregation inherited. However, a declining membership and a dwindling support base compound the basic problem of the building. The congregation grays; more and more of the folks live on fixed retirement incomes. Utility costs soar, especially heating fuel. Plumbing and wiring may need major work. Add to that the subtle and unnoticed changes in the congregation's needs: Present membership requires handicapped access, a sound system for the hearing impaired, and a health department code-approved kitchen. Throw in the cost of tuning that old pipe organ and—whew! But like single-factor low esteem, multiple-factor low esteem may disappear with the completion of a new facility or a major renovation project.

Tremendous damage results from *mistaking symptoms for causes*. Not long ago I received a church newsletter that described a congregation's cash shortage. Their pastoral salary costs had risen steadily while most of their aging membership struggled to survive on fixed incomes or died. Yet I knew they had always been committed people who gave until it hurt in support of their church. Because there was not enough to pay all the salaries, operating expenses, denominational askings, and benevolences, the pastor and finance chairperson relentlessly printed "red ink" notices in the newsletter and weekly worship bulletin. The pastor's letter said, "If we were *more committed* [italics mine], we wouldn't have this financial problem." That pastor had mistaken a *symptom*—cash shortage—for a *cause*—lack of commitment. Actually they were devoted and deserved to be told that. Without acknowledging and affirming their commitment, the church's esteem would be severely damaged. Congregational esteem might be improved by hiring a different pastor, or at least with the current pastor changing his attitude and behavior. Yet the primary issue probably is not the pastoral leadership. Instead it is the factors stemming from the church's changed financial and membership base that should be scrutinzed.

The pastor of a 200-member church near New York City told me the congregation faced the hardest financial crunch and membership decline in its twenty-five-year history. At the urging of this loving and capable pastor, they considered a shared-minister arrangement with a nearby church of similar size experiencing the same difficulties. Folks at that church submitted to the plan; in their resignation, they spoke from their heads and not from their hearts. Their rationalization was convincing, but their voices told another story. They sounded glum, depressed, and spiritless.

"If we don't yoke with the other church, we've got to close our doors," they told me. Yet when I asked them about their financial problems, nearly everyone said, "Things are tight, but we've been in these situations before and have come through it. But the pastor insists things are desperate and we've got to yoke as soon as possible if we're to save this church."

In short, the pastor had *misinterpreted* the signs. Yes, there *was* a cash flow problem and the denominational askings *were* behind for several years. "Look, we still managed to pay two-thirds last year and three-quarters this year," the treasurer said proudly. Yes, there *was* a noticeable membership decline—a couple of key families had left the area and two other active couples approached retirement.

Unfortunately, several esteem-boosting factors were overlooked because of the "four M" focus on institutional survival: money, members, mortar, and maintenance.

First, *sharing a pastor or closing the doors were not the only two options.* The people jumped too quickly in their decision to share a pastor. Many churches mistakenly believe that being a full-time church means employing a full-time minister. One solid option is employing a part-time staff to tackle a temporarily difficult situation. This solution was never considered, though it should have been.

Second, *the strength of the congregation was sorely underestimated.* The congregation demonstrated a positive track record spanning twenty-five years. The church was trying hard, a fact that was overlooked. The pastor, not wanting to disappoint the denominational supervisors, saw the payments from a different perspective than the church treasurer saw them. The pastor emphasized the shortage: In his estimation, the church's cup was one-third empty.

Third, *new members were coming in.* Young people with children were attracted to the pastor, the congregation, and the programs. The visitor-turned-member ratio was amazing, with newcomers attending from a twenty-mile radius beyond the old surrounding neighborhood. However, this statistic was missed.

Talk about misreading the signs! This congregation was not sliding downhill; instead, it was entering a cycle of renewal. It would have been a huge mistake to share a pastor with another congregation of the same size. Losing *that particular pastor*—one of the keys to that parish's renewal—would have been terrible.

The people pointed out that the pastor, even though acting out of love and concern, had created a congregational *faith crisis.* They objected.

"Don't you have faith in us? Do we have faith in our membership? Doesn't our track record indicate we're trying? Can we have faith in you as our leader, or will you bail out when things get tough?" The pastor realized he had pushed the panic button. He repented and publicly asked the congregation's forgiveness, and a healthy pastor-parish relationship was restored.

By uplifting the congregation's strengths and clarifying issues, church esteem turned upward and the people soared on eagles' wings. Two years later the same pastor was still in place, many improvements had been made, programming was stronger, bills were paid, mission and outreach increased higher than ever, and the church was awaiting the arrival of a new steeple.

There is a strange paradox I have discovered about small churches. The people think they do not try hard enough when in fact many try too hard. They strain to compete according to the models of a different size organization or large church. It is not uncommon for Family and Pastoral churches to adopt a Program church approach to activities. They do so for several reasons. Perhaps the incoming pastor is inclined that way and "feels" Program-sized behavior is the way to be a "good" church. Perhaps newer members enter from Program church backgrounds and bring those expectations. Then there is the dominant culture's obsession with competition. This approach frequently leads to burnout, a sense of failure, and low church esteem. Many small churches struggle to fulfill impossible expectations, especially in establishing programs. The people weary. Down on themselves, they minimize their natural strengths and maximize their weaknesses. A small congregation that overexerts itself often accomplishes nothing but frustration.

My advice? Do not strive, particularly if you play someone else's game according to their rules. Do not try to be someone else. Be yourself and be comfortable with the church God has called you to be. Pick or design those programs that are right for your specific context and that will best use your congregation's gifts and talents. Be unique and different part of the time; other times, borrow ideas from other churches if these will work for you. Try what one pastor calls "cheap thrills"— programs that are *high visibility* with *low energy drain*. Publicize, celebrate, and offer visible appreciation.

Keep in mind that the following ideas may be morale boosters that generate *temporary* positive esteem. This may be all that some churches need at the time. "Cheap thrills" programs are not meant to replace important needs, such as tackling the church's self-esteem. Understandably, serious issues will require more time and specialized assistance.

The Programmatic Approach without Being a Program Church: Eight Ideas to Raise Esteem

1. An eighty-three member New York church has an average attendance of twenty-five. More than three-quarters of the worshipers are retired, many in their seventies and eighties. The group cannot engage in outreach activities that require high energy, but when they discovered they were photogenic, they came up with a novel idea. Each week after worship the congregation poses before a Polaroid. They then send the photo—along with a card signed by everyone—to a different person selected for the week. They often choose a person who is not a church member. These *Card-n-Photos* have been sent to a college student; to the oldest woman in the denomination (age 117); to a high-school scholarship winner; to the local Fireman of the Year; to a 78-year old Maine woman earning her bachelor's degree; and to the widow of a past minister of the church. They call their endeavor a *ministry of hospitality*. What a suitable project for this particular congregation.

2. The same congregation felt that putting on regular fundraising suppers was too strenuous for most members. They decided they could manage at least one special supper each year. They hosted a Volunteer Fire Department *Appreciation Banquet* for the local eighty-member fire company and auxiliary—the first in its one-hundred year history. Decorations were creative, speeches short, and the pot roast was delicious. These two ideas were simple, appropriate, highly visible activities that helped the church feel good about itself.

3. A 240-member Vermont church collects food for the local emergency food pantry by hosting a *Shopping Bag Sunday*. Two Sundays in advance, each worshiper is handed a brown paper shopping bag on the way out of worship. Each bag has stapled to it a list of the most-needed items for the food shelf. People are asked to return them—filled with food—on Shopping Bag Sunday. The bags are carried to the altar

during the first hymn; there is a powerful, visible impact on the worshipers, especially on the visitors. They see faith put into action.

4. The same church celebrates World Communion Sunday each year with a *Bread Fest*. Worshipers are asked to bring a loaf of their favorite homemade bread or their favorite spreads. What a tasty assortment of breads ranging from zucchini, carrot, pumpkin, to cranberry, topped with homemade or store-bought jams and jellies! After a brief service in the sanctuary, everyone proceeds to the fellowship hall for the communion service. One of the donated loaves is used for the Lord's Supper; afterwards everyone samples the many breads and spreads. For several years World Communion Bread Fest and Shopping Bag Sunday were combined. The food went to stock the local pantry; the leftover breads were delivered to the soup kitchen; and a special offering was forwarded to a denominational mission. These activities are highly visible, contextually appropriate, produce high value with minimal energy investment, and boost esteem tremendously.

5. A Massachusetts church collected new and used *jigsaw puzzles* to be used by a cancer treatment center. The puzzles were placed on a table in the waiting room so patients awaiting treatment could work alone or together to pass the time. The project has high value for low energy output.

6. Many churches have discovered the value of *pew Bibles*. Worshipers can read the morning Scripture together, silently or aloud. Just buying the Bibles can be a worthwhile way to raise congregational self-esteem. The American Bible Society sells hardcover pew Bibles in many versions for a nominal cost (about five dollars each). Asking members to purchase one or more Bibles is a simple way to cover costs. Each copy can be dedicated in memory or in honor of someone by using glue-in bookplates. A special dedication service is appropriate.

7. Another church set up a *mission and outreach tree*, a terrific visual aid that raised awareness and esteem. Someone found a plywood tree that had been used as a sign for the annual Christmas bazaar. People created leaves that were placed on the tree with thumbtacks, with each leaf describing a mission or outreach of the church. Once those leaves began covering the tree, everyone was amazed at how much the church was doing without their realization. People added even more leaves to the tree, noting that the congregation had three people on the five-person local school board and citing the number of its members on the boards of

nonprofit agencies. Both of these are noteworthy examples of God's service.

8. Another church recognized that many people could not afford a Palm Sunday ham dinner, a tradition shared by many of the parishioners. So the church sponsored a *Hams-for-the-Haven* Palm Sunday food drive. (The Haven is the local shelter that also dispenses emergency food and holiday baskets to the needy.) During Lent, the season of sacrifice, worshipers were reminded to buy a canned ham to bring on Palm Sunday. During the offertory worshipers were asked to bring the hams and their regular morning offerings to the altar. The congregation, which averaged sixty worshipers, had ninety folks in attendance that day. The food offering was generous: Sixty-two hams were left at the altar.

There are countless projects that bring congregations together without overtaxing resources. Many of these are simple and fun and at the same time raise small church esteem. Try a community walk to fight hunger or a blanket Sunday to fight the cold. Or send much needed used clothing to one of the Appalachian missions your denomination supports. Have a silly awards night at church, recognizing behind-the-scenes workers (what I call "Holy Hoopla"). Get a printer to run off a community birthday and anniversary calendar. Support a missionary or a seminarian.

If low or mediocre esteem is an issue for your church:

— *Do not judge* your church by another congregation's standards for success.

— *Do not jump to conclusions*, mistaking symptoms for causes. Beware of faulty perceptions.

— *Do not try too hard.* Maybe it is easier than you think;

— *Be unique*, but borrow ideas that work.

— *Test out* a few high visibility ideas that do not drain energy ("cheap thrills"). Keep the projects simple, easy, and context appropriate.

— *Celebrate*, appreciate, make visible.

— *Pat yourselves on the back* more often.

— *Have fun!*[1]

Although the program approach is not a complete strategy for raising small church esteem, it can be part of a coordinated strategy. At first glance it may seem to be cosmetic, but it can boost morale leading to an examination of the root causes of low esteem. It must be noted that if a small church in its unique context continually engages in the *wrong* programs, the consequence will be low esteem.

Questions for Consideration

1. List your church's various program ideas.

2. Which ideas are size and context appropriate?

3. Which programs seem difficult to accomplish or are frustrating?

4. Which are stale ideas from a previous time or from a previous pastor's tenure? Are there ticklish feelings associated with evaluating them and possibly discontinuing them? How do you deal with those conflicting feelings and opinions?

5. Which program ideas are the most fun and which are the most satisfying?

6. What new idea was tried? Did it take hold?

7. How do you pat ourselves on the back, recognize, celebrate, and appreciate?

8. What are the forums that give all a chance to introduce and toss around new ideas without prejudgment? How can the church ensure the continuity of such forums?

9. Brainstorm ideas from other churches, organizations, and places. Which ones might work in your church?

10. What might be some "cheap thrills" (high visibility/low energy drain) ideas for your congregation to try, to succeed at, and to celebrate as a way of raising esteem and morale?

11. How are programs evaluated after they have been tried? How does the church decide to discontinue programs? Who decides and by what process?

12. What skills and talents are already present in your church that might be utilized in featured programs or in mission and outreach? (During the

monthly fellowship time following worship, can someone take and record blood pressures? Can the cooks each contribute a crockpot of homemade soup for a Soupathon?)

13. What would happen if the church encouraged everyone to work in teams or small covenant groups for a year, with each group seeking a way to use their gifts to design a program or mission and outreach program?

Additional Ideas [HAR]

Hold a *campfire night*. This is a storytelling event—a time to remember.
It is a great way to share your church's story, especially with new people
being adopted into the life of your congregation. Life is not lived on
Cloud Nine, so be sure to include accounts of adversity. This helps all to
understand how your small church weathers the storms of life.

Write *articles* about your small church for your denomination's
newsletter or for one of the half-dozen small church newsletters around
the country.[2] Every church needs to feel connected to other churches.

Hold *neighborhood events*—chicken barbecues, ice cream socials,
strawberry festivals—to become acquainted with your neighbors. Tell
them your story, using slides, video, drama; invite them to share their
expectations of the church. This can even work in areas where the neighbors are mostly business folks. A chance to meet people from other
backgrounds is a positive way to build community.

Hold *appreciation events* that honor faithfulness to some aspect of
church life.[3] Thank you notes are important when individuals make
monetary gifts to your church's memorial fund or even to those who do
not regularly participate in your church. Even Jesus expected to be
thanked (the ten lepers were cleansed, but only one returned to give
thanks).

Get involved in *mission and outreach events* that incarnate God's
love for the world. Invite others to join with your church family as you
express that mission (e.g., Habitat for Humanity, Blanket Sundays,
CROP Walks).

Encourage *good stewardship* and remind individuals to remember
the church in their wills. Our resources, however, consist of more than
money. Stewardship is a way of life that includes the earth and how we
use it, the work we do, the time we invest, the study habits we establish,
and finally, the dedication of our retirement years.

Practice hospitality. Remember, the small church has the capacity
to be inclusive rather than exclusive. By its very structure, the small
church allows intimacy rather than just acquaintance relationships.
Individuals can be adopted into the life of the small church; they can be
accepted as the persons God has created them to be. In addition, the
small church has the ability to welcome the stranger.[4]

Finally, ask your *denomination* to offer events that relate specifically to the life of the small church. Such events might even cross denominational lines, as small churches share common universals. There are some successful programs such as the American Baptists' creation, "Seeds of Renewal Schools," which aims to enhance small church vitality. Bangor Theological Seminary's Small Church Leadership Program assists student pastors in the development of skills needed for small church ministry. The Small Church Advanced Training Institute set up by the Episcopal Diocese of Virginia is being replicated in four other dioceses. The Missouri School of Religion's Small Church Program has developed an ecumenical Small Church Project Team that is doing wonderful things together. One-time events are popping up all over the country. Steve Burt and Tony Pappas spend lots of time on the road planning and keynoting regional and national small church events. These leaders are accessible and easy to talk to. To get a feel for what is being done, check out *The Small Church Newsletter* Steve edits (P.O. Box 104685, Jefferson City, MO 65110-4685) or *The Five Stones* newsletter Tony edits (P.O. Box D2, Block Island, RI 02807).

CONCLUSION

Raising small church esteem is a tall order because of the complexity of congregational identity and its related health. Consider for example the many areas referred to in previous chapters: identity, morale, leadership, board and committee structures, physical plant, decision making, education, mission and outreach, program, newcomer assimilation, conflict resolution, communications, size-related organizational dynamics, relationship to denomination, denominational leadership, context, history, community image, church peer pressures, institutional maintenance, seminary curricula, and more. These areas are so intertwined that to separate each element for analysis is like trying to untie the Gordian Knot.

However all these items can be tackled and small church esteem can be raised. We have witnessed it in our case studies and in plenty of real life situations. Furthermore, we have seen success in places we least expected. It is true that small church esteem probably will not be raised overnight, but we can boost it one step at a time. We can address the issues in several major areas.

First, we must begin helping people—pastors, lay persons, denominational and judicatory executives, and seminary faculty—to understand that the small church is a unique entity and to respect that distinction. Congregations with modest sizes differ from larger churches.

There are many excellent print resources available today with more being developed for the 1990s. We are also beginning to create some instructive videotapes. The concepts shared in these print and video resources are neither technical nor obscure. In fact, the materials are practical and accessible to users ranging from pastors to small church laity. Suitable places in which to discuss and wrestle with the issues highlighted in the resources include seminary classes, regional training events for laity and clergy, and cluster or in-church discussion groups. Education is vital: People need to understand the organism of which they are a part. Any of the users can take the initiative—it need not be relegated to the seminary or to the denominational program staff.

Second, we must assist individual small churches with the identity issue. Society was changed rapidly. Today many churches know who they *were*, but few know who they *are*. Confusion abounds.

"Church check-ups" or weekend "identity assessments" (as Hazel described in the Hillview case study) can work wonders. These sessions steer the local church away from its focus on deficiencies and guide it to view its strengths and assets. Identity assessments not only give churches data, the process affirms a church. Invariably, a congregation's self-esteem is raised by the end of that weekend. The positive energy and the assessment information can then be utilized to put the church in forward motion, full of hope for its future.

How in the world can so few consultants work with the tens of thousands of small churches requiring this kind of work?

One approach is a pilot Small Church Program developed by the Missouri School of Religion (MSR). Six assessments are scheduled for the year in churches of different denominations. Members of MSR's ecumenical Small Church Project Team (lay and clergy volunteers) then prepare to work as on-site consultant-trainees alongside a senior consultant. They learn about size-relative organizational dynamics and engage in basic consultant preparation (e.g., congregational studies and issue identification). Trainees participate in the assessments, help write reports, and provide follow-up. Eventually the Team members themselves conduct assessments in two's and three's without the on-site supervisor. Groups from other parts of the country are already asking whether they can receive intensive training. Afterwards, they intend to set up their own ecumenical small church project teams.

The American Baptist "Seeds of Renewal Program," recently field tested in Rhode Island and upstate New York, approaches the church identity issue from the angle of leadership development. Pastors and several laity representatives from a handful of small churches join with facilitators for a four-day retreat. During their time together they worship, study, and enjoy fellowship. They also learn about small church dynamics and systems. Hazel Roper, Tony Pappas, and a myriad of participants now attest to the Seeds of Renewal Program's dramatic power for revitalizing individuals and churches. In fact, it has proven so successful that a part-time coordinator was hired to schedule and organize more Seeds of Renewal retreats.

Another area relevant to the identity issue in small churches is the development of updated mission statements that consider the congregation's present context. There are workbooks available from denominational publishing houses, and some judicatory or program staff are able and ready to assist. Keep in mind that the process may be more valuable than the product.

A third major area calls for a redefinition of "success." Many small churches have yet to learn that they do not have to keep up with their larger cousins. They need to do what they *can do*, rather than to struggle with what they cannot or should not do. A church that has experienced shrinkage cannot continue to generate and staff programs at the level it once did. Now it must find activities and missions suited to its new size. "Graying" small churches may have to admit that "we don't do youth ministry well any more, but we *can do* (you name it) pretty well." Sharing resources and program suggestions will help—ideas that are size-, context-, age-, and energy-appropriate. Creating and communicating these resources should become our priority.

Fourth, we must begin to redefine *clergy success*—incorporating the viewpoints of both ministers and the denominations. A host of issues arise from this topic: "climbing the ladder" of size, equitable salaries not tied to a size gradient, stroking, status, and other "benefits."

Fifth, we have to rethink ministry deployment. How can we best benefit the churches as well as the ministers? Vital areas to explore are found in the following questions: "Whose needs are served when we create multiple-church parishes?" and "What about a bivocational licensed (not ordained) minister of another denomination for this small church?" A corollary might be: "What about educating nonordained ministers ecumenically?" In other words, why not train licensed lay pastors and lay speakers of several denominations in the same regional school or retreat? A case in point for cross-denominational deployment is the Eastern Vermont Ecumenical Lay Preaching Team. They rescued several small churches by providing pulpit supply.

Sixth, we need to develop our conflict management and mediation skills, starting with the leadership and then working with small church laity. Skills are needed in the areas of consensus decision making, "getting to yes," and creating win/win situations. At all costs, we need to avoid the distressing atmosphere of win/lose or lose/lose that will only drive people away.[1]

Seventh, we must recognize that evangelism might lose something in the translation for the small church. Among other things, it may mean *making disciples* rather than *making new members;* it may mean changing slowly in a being-rather-than-doing approach to evangelism. Inevitably, the small church will be pressured because of its numerical decline. The negative reactions of the denominational front office and the church growth movement will hardly produce in small churches the high esteem and sense of self-worth so desperately needed. Faithfulness, not numerical growth, needs to be the yardstick. Wherever we find it, faithfulness needs to be celebrated.

Finally, we have to "raise up" the small church, celebrate it, offer more local and denominational awards, express appreciation, and print more articles about its successes. We need to stop hiding this great light—the faithful, effective, people-affirming small church—under a bushel. Indeed, as David Ray aptly states in his book title, *small churches are the right size.*[2]

Our book is not the definitive word on small church esteem. In fact we have probably raised more questions than we have answered. But we do hope our contribution will prove to be meaningful, helpful, and sufficiently stimulating. May many of us join together to address the urgent issue of raising small church esteem.

NOTES

Introduction

1. Carl S. Dudley, *Making the Small Church Effective* (Nashville: Abingdon, 1978), Chapter Two.

2. Lyle E. Schaller, *Looking in the Mirror: Self-Appraisal in the Local Church* (Nashville: Abingdon, 1984), Chapter One.

3. For more on defining "small church" experientially see Steve Burt, *Activating Leadership in the Small Church: Clergy and Laity Working Together*, "Small Church in Action Series," edited by Douglas Alan Walrath (Valley Forge, PA: Judson Press, 1988), Chapter One.

4. Marsha Sinetar, *Self-Esteem Is Just an Idea We Have About Ourselves* (New York: Paulist Press, 1990), 5-7, 11-13. Sinetar's delightful and profound 80-page book resembles a children's picture book though it is designed also for adults. The text is available in both English and Spanish.

5. Ibid., 14-29.

6. Ibid., 71-75.

Chapter 1 *(none)*

Chapter 2

1. See Daniel Buttry, *Bringing Your Church Back to Life: Beyond Survival Mentality* (Valley Forge: Judson Press, 1988), Chapter One, for identification of the symptoms of survival mentality.

2. See "Two Cultures Experience People Helping People," *The American Baptist* (November-December 1986):44 for a detailed account.

3. See Carl S. Dudley and Douglas Alan Walrath, *Developing Your Small Church's Potential*, "Small Church in Action Series," edited by Douglas Alan Walrath (Valley Forge, PA: Judson Press, 1988), Chapters One and Two, for a thorough treatment of the connection between a church's context and its ministry.

4. See James C. Fenhagen, *Mutual Ministry* (New York: Seabury, 1977), Chapters Two and Seven, for a detailed description of mutual ministry and its impact on the life of the church.

5. See Elisabeth Kubler-Ross, *On Death and Dying* (New York: Macmillan, 1969), 38-137, for a thorough analysis of the stages of grief.

6. See Michael J. Christensen, *City Streets, City People: A Call for Compassion* (Nashville: Abingdon, 1988), Chapters One and Two, for an understanding of the implications of loss. See also Frank and Janet Farrell, with Edward Wakin, *Trevor's Place: The Story of the Boy Who Brings Hope to the Homeless* (San Francisco: Harper & Row, 1990), to learn how a young boy can respond to human need with a vision put into action.

7. See Martin F. Saarinen, *The Life Cycle of a Congregation* (Washington, DC: The Alban Institute, 1990) for understanding identity crises in relation to the life cycles of a church (birth, infancy, prime, maturity, aristocracy, bureaucracy, and death).

8. See Robert Dale, *To Dream Again* (Nashville: Broadman Press, 1981), Chapters Eight and Nine, for a detailed examination of elements in the church life-cycle that are warning signs of low esteem.

9. See Denham Grierson, *Transforming a People of God* (Melbourne: The Joint Board of Christian Education of Australia and New Zealand, 1984), Chapter Ten, for a look at "openings for ministry" in relation to worship, mission, education, authority. Appendix Three is a tool to assist the process.

10. David R. Ray, *Small Churches Are the Right Size* (New York: Pilgrim Press, 1982), 169. The book went out of print in 1990, but Ray is revising and expanding it. Pilgrim Press plans to issue the expanded version under a new title, *All About Small Churches* (tentative), in fall 1992. Adapted with permission for readers to copy this instrument for church use.

Chapter 3

1. For an excellent analysis of this size-related "Peter principle," see Roy Oswald, "How to Minister Effectively in Family, Pastoral, Program, and Corporate Sized Churches," *Action Information* (Washington, DC: The Alban Institute, March-April 1991).

2. Arlen J. Rothauge, *Sizing Up a Congregation for New Member Ministry* (New York: The Education for Mission and Ministry Office, The Episcopal Church Center, updated). Rothauge's 38-page booklet is being reprinted in 1991, and is excellent for discussion groups. Another excellent resource for discussion groups that uses the Rothauge-size models is the 74-page booklet *Bonds of Belonging: Pathways to Discipleship for Church Members*, by Donald F. LaSuer and L. Ray Sells (Nashville: Discipleship Resources, 1986).

3. Lyle E. Schaller, *Looking in the Mirror: Self-Appraisal in the Local Church* (Nashville: Abingdon, 1984).

4. We prefer using *average worship attendance* as a way of focusing on the entity Rothauge identifies as the Family Church. His numerical guide in *Sizing Up a Congregation* is 0-50 active members. In his writings and in his workshops, Schaller uses as his numerical figure 0-35/40 at worship. We use 2-35 as a rough guideline.

5. For a fascinating look at role-playing in small churches, see Anthony G. Pappas, *Entering the World of the Small Church* (Washington, DC: The Alban Institute, 1988). Pappas' comparisons of the small church to the folk society described by Robert Redfield in his article "The Folk Society" are helpful.

6. Schaller, *Looking in the Mirror*, Chapter One.

7. Again, we prefer using a figure based on average attendance (35-90). Rothauge's Pastoral Church model in *Sizing Up a Congregation* suggests 50-150 active members. Schaller lists 35-100 at worship in *Looking in the Mirror*.

8. Rothauge, *Sizing Up a Congregation*, 15.

9. Schaller, *Looking in the Mirror*, Chapter One.

10. Rothauge uses 150-350 active members as his base in *Sizing Up a Congregation*. Schaller suggests 100-175 at worship in *Looking in the Mirror*. We prefer 90-150 at worship as our guideline.

11. Ibid., Chapter One.

12. For a helpful key to a church's governing board and the wide

range of members' expectations (and pressures) on the pastor, see "The Card Game" in Steve Burt's *Activating Leadership in the Small Church: Clergy and Laity Working Together*, "Small Church in Action Series," edited by Douglas Alan Walrath (Valley Forge, PA: Judson Press, 1988), 101-03.

13. For amplification of the single-cell dynamics concept, see Carl S. Dudley, *Unique Dynamics of the Small Church* (Washington, DC: The Alban Institute, 1977).

Chapter 4

1. See Walter Cook, *Send Us a Minister . . . Any Minister Will Do* (Rockland, ME: Courier-Gazette, 1978), for stories of small churches served by Bangor Theological Seminary's student ministers over the years. The book is available from the Bangor Seminary bookstore, 300 Union Street, Bangor, ME 04401.

2. Carl S. Dudley, *Making the Small Church Effective* (Nashville: Abingdon, 1978), 71-74. Although we are suggesting "companion" as a less charged image today, there is still much to be gained by reading Dudley's treatment of the "lover" image.

3. See David R. Ray, *Small Churches Are the Right Size* (New York: Pilgrim Press, 1982), Chapter Two, for a theology of smallness.

4. Lyle E. Schaller, *The Small Church Is Different* (Nashville: Abingdon, 1982), 60.

5. See Lyle E. Schaller, *The Pastor and the People* (Nashville: Abingdon Press, 1986), Chapter Four, for additional information regarding intentional interims.

6. The American Baptist Churches of New York State, in cooperation with The Alban Institute, have created the New Pastor's Institute as a way to bridge the gap between the seminary and the local church. This three-year program is a developed combination of the peer-learning model and the apprentice model, with the mentor being a pastor with leadership training skills. Yearly retreats bring the entire group together with denominational staff. A key player in the model is the Pastoral Relations Committee (Ministry Support Team), which assists the pastor in identifying needs that must be addressed for effective leadership in the church. They also monitor applications of their Institute training. Many denominations use similar processes to assist recent

93

seminary graduates in making the transition from seminary to the local church.

In June 1991, under the direction of its Small Church Leadership Program, Bangor Theological Seminary in Maine offered an ecumenical "Orientation for Pastors of Rural and Small Town Churches."

The Missouri School of Religion's ecumenical Small Church Project Team, in cooperation with the Heartland Network (United Methodist Church) and the Office of Creative Ministries (Columbia, Missouri), joined with Judicatories to offer a "Newcomer Pastor" retreat in Nebraska City, Nebraska (for Nebraska, Kansas, Missouri, Iowa, Illinois, Oklahoma, and Dakotas pastors). This type of planning fosters interdenominational cooperation as well as ownership of the events.

In 1990 and again in 1991 the Episcopal Diocese of Virginia, under the direction of Rev. Robert Hansel, developed and successfully tested a new training model, The Small Church Advanced Training Institute. This method brings together small church rectors (included in the invitation are recent seminary graduates) over a period of six to eight months, meeting two days each month in retreats designed for training. The small group of 8-14 rectors interacts with a variety of "experts" in the small church field; each participant engages in interviews with trained counselors before and after each monthly session. This program was so well received that it is being replicated in four other dioceses.

Chapter 5

1. Norris Smith, "Forced Termination: Scope and Response" *Search*, vol. 21, no. 1, (Fall 1990):6.

2. See Speed B. Leas, *Leading Your Church Through Conflict* (Washington, DC: The Alban Institute, 1985), Chapters 3, 7-10, for a detailed description of the elements of conflicts and the strategies for resolution.

3. Donald W. DeMott, *Each Teach Two* (Geneseo, NY: High Falls Publications, 1991), 14-17. Another outstanding guidebook that offers theory and strategies is *Getting to Yes: Negotiating Agreement Without Giving In* by Roger Fisher, William Ury, et al. (Boston: Houghton Mifflin, 1981); also available in paperback (New York: Penguin, 1983).

4. See Speed B. Leas, *Leadership and Conflict*, "Creative

Leadership Series," edited by Lyle E. Schaller (Nashville: Abingdon, 1990), Chapter Nine, for a more detailed description of this dynamic.

5. Anthony G. Pappas, *Entering the World of the Small Church: A Guide for Leaders* (Washington, DC: The Alban Institute, 1988), 32.

6. Edwin H. Friedman *Generation to Generation: Family Process in Church and Synagogue*, "The Guilford Family Therapy Series," edited by Alan S. Gurman (New York: The Guilford Press, 1985), 46-47, 78-99, 193-210, 219.

7. *Alcoholics Anonymous Comes of Age: A Brief History of A.A.* (New York: Alcoholics Anonymous World Services, Inc., 1957), 161.

8. Keith Huttenlocker, *Conflict and Caring* (Grand Rapids: Zondervan, 1988), 73.

9. See Douglas Alan Walrath, *Frameworks: Patterns for Living and Believing Today* (New York: Pilgrim Press, 1987), Chapters Three and Five, for a thorough analysis of the role diversity plays in the life of the church.

10. Use Kathryn Choy-Wong, *Covenant Prayer Group Manual* (Valley Forge, PA: American Baptist Church Prayer and Community Development, 1988), to assist in the creation of covenant prayer groups that reflect the diversity of your church.

Chapter 6

1. Edwin H. Friedman, *Generation to Generation* (New York: The Guilford Press, 1985). Friedman looks at how family systems affect the dynamics and life of congregations. It is especially applicable to the life of the small church. For a brief introduction to Friedman's work, see "A Family Systems Expert Talks About Congregational Leadership," an interview conducted by Celia Allison Hahn, *Action Information* (Washington, DC: The Alban Institute, May-June 1985).

2. See Steve Burt, "Small Churches Helping Small Churches: The Eastern Vermont Lay Preaching Group," *Five Stones* (Summer 1988).

3. See Davida Foy Crabtree, *The Empowering Church: How One Congregation Supports Lay People's Ministries in the World* (Washington, DC: The Alban Institute, 1989) for a more in-depth analysis of why and how to do this. She and her congregation also realized the church's committee structure was set up for mostly

institutional maintenance (service to the church), when what the people needed was a structure to unleash their energies outwardly in service to the world. To accomplish that, the church had to become an equipping station, preparing the saints for ministry.

4. For information on these inductive Bible study materials, contact Neighborhood Bible Studies, Inc., Box 222, Dobbs Ferry, NY 10522-0222.

5. For additional ideas regarding education groups, see Steve Burt, "Adult Education Groups: 10 Ideas for Any Size Church," *Church Educator* (July 1990), or *Baptist Leader* (Winter 1990-91).

6. See Anthony Pappas, *Money, Motivation and Mission in the Small Church*, "Small Church in Action Series," edited by Douglas Alan Walrath (Valley Forge, PA: Judson Press, 1989), 56-76, for more strategies on fundraising. Regarding the re-establishment of the turkey supper programs at White River Methodist, Pappas writes: "Utilize patterned behaviors already within the memory and activity repertoire of the congregation," 61.

7. See also Steve Burt, "Ten Good Reasons for Church Suppers," *Your Church* (May-June 1986).

8. For more ideas, see Steve Burt, "Ten Mission and Outreach Ideas for the Small Church," *The Small Church Newsletter* (June 1991).

9. See Steve Burt, "Breathe Life into Those Litanies," *Church Worship* (December 1990), or "How to Write Litanies," *Your Church* (November-December 1984), for examples and ideas.

10. For more on developing user friendly bulletins, see Steve Burt, "Is Your Church's Bulletin User Friendly?" *Church Worship*, (May 1991). For more on user friendly worship services, see Steve Burt, *Activating Leadership in the Small Church: Clergy and Laity Working Together* (Valley Forge, PA: Judson Press, 1988), 83-84.

11. See Steve Burt, "World Communion Brown Bags and Bread Fest," *Church Worship* (August 1990), for detailed information on "Shopping Bag Hunger Response."

12. Steve Burt, "Our Church Cares: 10 Ways to Show It," *Your Church* (September-October 1985).

13. Steve Burt, "World Communion," *The Interpreter* (July-August 1988), or *Five Stones* (Fall 1989).

14. See footnote 11.

15. The exercise which was used can be found in Lyle E.

Schaller, *The Pastor and the People: Building a New Partnership for Effective Ministry* (Nashville: Abingdon, 1973), 46-47. It is most helpful in revealing to a governing board a certain congregation's impossible assumptions and underscores the pastor's difficulty in realistically assessing membership's expectations; this book is less helpful in the area of setting priorities. A variation of the tool is "The Card Game," found in Steve Burt, *Activating Leadership in the Small Church: Clergy and Laity Working Together* (Valley Forge, PA: Judson Press), 101-103.

Chapter 7

1. Up to this point, the chapter closely follows Steve Burt, "Pump It Up! Options for the Small Church," *Church Herald* (January 1991).

2. Such national small church newsletters include *The Small Church Newsletter*, edited by Steve Burt, Missouri School of Religion, PO Box 104685, Jefferson City, MO 65110-4685; *The Five Stones*, edited by Tony Pappas, First Baptist Church, P.O. Box D2, Block Island, RI 02807; *United Methodist Rural Fellowship Bulletin*, edited by Roger E. Armstrong, c/o Carr Memorial United Methodist Church, 909 Wisconsin, Pine Bluff, AR 71601; "The Small Church Page," edited by Sally and Fred Page, in the Synod of the Sun Edition of *News of the Presbyterian Church* (USA), P.O. Box 697, Fordyce, AR 71742; *The Armenian: For Churches that Are Small in Size Only*, a publication of United Methodist Town and Country Ministries, edited by Ken Calhoun, P.O. Box 216, Hooks, TX 75561.

3. See Steve Burt, *Activating Leadership in the Small Church: Clergy and Laity Working Together*, "Small Church in Action Series," edited by Douglas Alan Walrath (Valley Forge, PA: Judson Press, 1988), especially Chapter Five, "Holy Hoopla and Making Love to the Congregation: Creating a Favorable Climate for Volunteers."

4. For additional program ideas see Steve Burt, *Activating Leadership*, Chapter Six, "What Can Our Small Church Do?" A wealth of ideas can be gleaned from John H. Krahn and Betty Jane Foster, *Ministry Ideabank* (Lima, OH: C.S.S. Publishing, 1981); *Ministry Ideabank No. 2* (Lima, OH: C.S.S. Publishing, 1986); and *Ministry Ideabank No. 3* (Lima, OH: C.S.S. Publishing, 1987).

Conclusion

1. For more on this, see *Getting to Yes: Negotiating Agreement Without Giving In,* by Roger Fisher, et al. (Boston: Houghton Mifflin, 1981).

2. David R. Ray, *Small Churches Are the Right Size* (New York: Pilgrim Press, 1982).

Books

Andrews, David, ed. *Ministry in the Small Church.* Kansas City, Mo.: Sheed and Ward, 1988.

————, et al. *Agenda for the Small Church: A Handbook for Rural Ministry.* Des Moines: National Catholic Rural Life Conference, 1988.

Berry, Wendell. *The Unsettling of America: Culture and Agriculture.* San Francisco: Sierra Club Books, 1977.

Bierly, Steve R. *Help for the Small Church Pastor: Unlocking the Potential of Your Congregation.* Grand Rapids, Mich.: Zondervan, 1995.

————. *How to Thrive as a Small-Church Pastor: A Guide to Spiritual and Emotional Well-Being.* Grand Rapids, Mich.: Zondervan, 1998.

Blunk, Henry. *The Smaller Church: Mission Study Guide.* Philadelphia: Westminster, 1981.

Brueggemann, Walter. *The Land.* Philadelphia: Fortress Press, 1977.

Burt, Steven E. "Choosing the Small Church Pastor." *Your Church* (September-October 1984).

———. "Our Church Cares: 10 Ways to Show It." *Your Church* (September-October 1985).

———. "Ten Good Reasons for Church Suppers." *Your Church* (May-June 1986).

———. *Activating Leadership in the Small Church: Clergy and Laity Working Together.* Small Church in Action Series. Edited by Douglas Alan Walrath. Valley Forge, Pa.: Judson Press, 1988.

———. "Small Churches Helping Small Churches: The Eastern Vermont Lay Preaching Group." *Five Stones* (Summer 1988).

———. "Help for Small Churches." *Resources* (Fall 1989). Reprinted in *The Small Church Newsletter* (March 1991).

———. "Can We Really Help the Small Church?" *New Horizons* (Winter 1990).

———. "Is Anyone Doing Anything for the Small Church?" *American Baptist Quarterly* (June 1990).

———. "Adult Discussion Groups: 10 Ideas for Any Size Church." *Church Educator* (July 1990). Reprinted in *The Baptist Leader* (Winter 1990-91); *Small Church Newsletter* (December 1991).

———. "Small Church Survival Kit." *The Small Church Newsletter* (November 1990).

———. "Pump It Up: Options for the Small Church." *Church Herald* (January 1991). Reprinted in *The Small Church Newsletter* (September 1991); *Action Information.* Washington D.C.: Alban Institute (July-August 1992); *Missionary Messenger* (January 1995); *United Church News,* Connecticut Conference wrap-around edition (February 1995).

———. "An Empty Pulpit: America's Impending Minister Shortage." *Rural Missouri* (March 1991). Reprinted in *The Small Church Newsletter* (June 1991); *The Arminian* (Fall 1991); *Church Worship* (January 1992).

———. "Small Wonder." *The Small Church Newsletter* (March 1991).

———. "Is Your Church's Bulletin User Friendly?" *Church Worship* (May 1991). Reprinted in *The Small Church Newsletter* (December 1991); *New Beginnings* (June 1992).

———. "Ten Mission and Outreach Ideas for the Small Church." *The Small Church Newsletter* (June 1991).

———. "Soup-a-thon Fundraiser for the Small Church." *The Arminian* (Summer 1991).

———. "Raising Small Church Esteem." *The Small Church Newsletter* (September 1991).

———. "A Small Church Network that Works." *New Horizons* (Fall 1991).

———. "Where's the Small Church Movement Going?" *The Small Church Newsletter* (March 1992).

———. "Why I Give Small Church Pep Talks." *Action Information.* Washington, D.C.: Alban Institute (April 1992).

———. "Dynamics of the Small Membership Church." *If I Were the Pastor of a Small Membership Church . . .* Tools for Ministry portfolio, Hinton Rural Life Center (August 1992).

———. "Small Churches: Living on 'People Time.'" *The Small Church Newsletter* (September 1992).

———. "Does Size Make a Difference?" *Congregations: The Alban Journal* (November-December 1992).

———. "What a Small Church You Have!" *Church Herald* (January 1995).

———. "Small Churches Can Do Mission." *Baptist Leader* (Spring 1997).

———. "Vermont Small Churches: Lights Hid Under a Bushel." *United Church News,* Vermont Conference wrap-around edition (September 1997).

Buttry, Daniel. *Bringing Your Church Back to Life: Beyond Survival Mentality.* Valley Forge, Pa.: Judson Press, 1988.

Carroll, Jackson W., Carl S. Dudley, and William McKinney, eds. *Handbook for Congregational Studies.* Nashville: Abingdon, 1986.

———, ed. *Small Churches Are Beautiful.* New York: Harper and Row, 1977.

Choy-Wong, Kathryn. *Covenant Prayer Group Manual.* Valley Forge, Pa.: American Baptist Prayer and Community Development, 1988.

Christenson, Michael J. *City Streets, City People: A Call for Compassion.* Nashville: Abingdon, 1988.

Chromey, Rick. *Youth Ministry in Small Churches.* Loveland, Colo.: Group Books, 1990.

Cook, Walter. *Send Us a Minister . . . Any Minister Will Do.* Rockland, Maine: Courier-Gazette, 1978. Write Bangor Seminary Bookstore, 300 Union Street, Bangor, Maine 04401.

Coote, Robert B., ed. *Mustard Seed Churches: Ministries in Small Churches.* Minneapolis: Augsburg Fortress, 1990.

Crabtree, Davida Foy. *The Empowering Church: How One Congregation Supports Lay People's Ministries in the World.* Washington, D.C.: The Alban Institute, 1989.

Crandall, Ronald K. *Turnaround Strategies for the Small Church.* Nashville: Abingdon Press, 1995.

————, and L. Ray Sells. *There's New Life in the Small Congregation! Why It Happens and How.* Nashville: Discipleship Resources, 1983.

Cronin, Deborah. *O for a Dozen Tongues to Sing: Music Ministry with Small Choirs.* Nashville: Abingdon Press, 1996.

Cushman, James. *Beyond Survival: Revitalizing the Small Church.* Louisville, Ky.: Presbyterian Church USA, 1981.

————. *Evangelism in the Small Church.* Decatur, Ga.: CTS Press, 1988.

————, et al. *New Times, New Call: A Manual of Pastoral Options for Small Churches.* Louisville, Ky.: Presbyterian Church USA, 1991.

Dalc, Robert. *To Dream Again.* Nashville: Broadman Press, 1981.

————. *Pastoral Leadership: A Handbook of Resources for Effective Congregational Leadership.* Nashville: Abingdon Press, 1986.

DeMott, Donald W. *Each Teach Two.* Genesee, N.Y.: High Falls Publications, 1991.

Diehl, William E. *Thank God It's Monday.* Philadelphia: Fortress Press, 1982.

————. *In Search of Faithfulness: Lesson from the Christian Community.* Philadelphia: Fortress Press, 1987.

Dudley, Carl S. *Unique Dynamics of the Small Church.* Washington, D.C.: The Alban Institute, 1977.

————. *Making the Small Church Effective.* Nashville: Abingdon Press, 1978.

————. *Where Have All Our People Gone? New Choices for Old Churches.* New York: Pilgrim Press, 1979.

————. *Basic Steps Toward Congregational Ministry: Guidelines and Models in Action.* Washington, D.C.: The Alban Institute, 1991.

————, and Douglas Alan Walrath. *Developing Your Small Church's Potential.* Small Church in Action Series. Edited by Douglas Alan Walrath. Valley Forge, Pa.: Judson Press, 1989.

Farley, Gary. "Fifteen Steps for Leading a Stable Rural Church Off the Plateau." *Net Results* (December 1991).

Farris, Lawrence. *Dynamics of Small Town Ministry.* Washington, D.C.: The Alban Institute, 2000.

Fenhagen, James C. *Mutual Ministry.* New York: Seabury, 1977.

Ferrell, Frank and Janet, with Edward Watkin. *Trevor's Place: The Story of a Boy Who Brings Hope to the Homeless.* San Francisco: Harper and Row, 1990.

Fisher, Roger, et al. *Getting to Yes: Negotiating Agreement Without Giving In.* Boston: Houghton Mifflin, 1981.

Flora, Cornelia, ed. *Rural Communities: Legacy and Change.* Boulder, Colo.: Westview Press, 1992.

Foltz, Nancy, ed. *Religious Education in the Small Membership Church.* Birmingham, Ala.: Religious Education Press, 1990.

————. *Caring for the Small Church: Insights from Women in Ministry.* Small Church in Action Series. Edited by Douglas Alan Walrath. Valley Forge, Pa.: Judson Press, 1994.

Friedman, Edwin H. "A Family Systems Expert Talks About Congregational Leadership." Interview by Celia Allison Hahn,

Action Information. Washington, D.C.: The Alban Institute (May-June 1985).

—. *Generation to Generation: Family Process in Church and Synagogue.* New York.: The Guilford Press, 1985.

Grierson, Denham. *Transforming a People of God.* Melbourne: The Joint Board of Christian Education of Australia and New Zealand, 1984.

Griffin, Richard. "A Guide for New Pastors." *Action Information.* Washington, D.C.: The Alban Institute (January-February 1991).

Griggs, Donald, and Judy McKay Walther. *Christian Education in the Small Church. Small Church in Action Series.* Edited by Douglas Alan Walrath. Valley Forge, Pa.: Judson Press, 1988.

Hargus, Clark. *Biblical Stewardship Principles: A Bible Study for Small Membership Congregations.* Indianapolis: Ecumenical Center for Stewardship Studies, 1991.

—. *Faithful, Hopeful, Loving.* Indianapolis: Ecumenical Center for Stewardship Studies, 1991.

—. "Small Church Health Test." *The Small Church Newsletter* (June 1991).

—. *Stewardship in the Small Membership Congregation.* Indianapolis: Ecumenical Center for Stewardship Studies, 1991.

Hopewell, James F. *Congregation: Stories and Structures.* Philadelphia: Fortress Press, 1987.

Huttenlocker, Keith. *Conflict and Caring.* Grand Rapids, Mich.: Zondervan, 1988.

Johnston, Jon, and Bill M. Sullivan, eds. *The Smaller Church in a SuperChurch Era.* Kansas City, Mo.: Beacon Hill Press of Kansas City, 1983.

Jung, Shannon, and Mary Agria. *Rural Congregational Studies: A Guide for Good Shepherds.* Minneapolis: Augsburg Publishing, 1997.

————, ed. *Rural Ministry: The Shape of the Renewal to Come.* Nashville: Abingdon Press, 1998.

Klassen, Ron, and John Koessler. *No Little Places: The Untapped Potential of the Small-Town Church.* Grand Rapids, Mich.: Baker Books, 1996.

Krahn, John H., and Betty Jane Foster. *Ministry Ideabank.* Lima, Ohio: C.S.S. Publishing, 1981.

————. *Ministry Ideabank No. 2.* Lima, Ohio: C.S.S. Publishing, 1986.

————. *Ministry Ideabank No. 3.* Lima, Ohio: C.S.S. Publishing, 1987.

Kubler-Ross, Elisabeth. *On Death and Dying.* New York: Macmillan, 1969.

Kunz, Marilyn, and Catherine Schell. *Mark.* Dobbs Ferry, N.Y.: Neighborhood Bible Studies, Inc., 1960.

LaSuer, Donald F., and L. Ray Sells. *Bonds of Belonging: Pathways to Discipleship for Church Members.* Nashville: Discipleship Resources, 1986.

Leas, Speed B., and Paul Kittlaus. *Church Fights: Managing Conflict in the Local Church.* Philadelphia: Westminster Press, 1978.

————. *The Lay Person's Guide to Conflict Management.* Washington, D.C.: The Alban Institute, 1979.

————. *Leading Your Church Through Conflict.* Washington, D.C.: The Alban Institute, 1985.

———. *Leadership and Conflict.* Nashville: Abingdon Press, 1990.

Lewis, C. Douglass. *Resolving Church Conflicts: A Case Study Approach for Local Congregations.* San Francisco: Harper and Row, 1981.

Madsen, Paul. *The Small Church: Valid, Vital, Victorious.* Valley Forge, Pa.: Judson Press, 1975.

Mann, Alice. *Can Our Church Live? Redeveloping Congregations in Decline.* Washington, D.C.: The Alban Institute, 2000.

Massa, Michael W., et al. *Ministry Resources: Planning Helps in Ten Program Areas for Congregations with Small Membership.* Minneapolis: Augsburg Publishing House, 1986.

McCarty, Doran. *Leading the Small Church.* Nashville: Broadman Press, 1991.

Olbert, Scott. "A Model for Understanding the Local Church." *Net Results* (June 1991).

Oswald, Roy M., and Speed B. Leas. *The Inviting Church: A Study of New Member Assimilation.* Washington, D.C.: The Alban Institute, 1987.

———. "How to Minister Effectively in Family, Pastoral, Program, and Corporate Sized Churches." *Action Information.* Washington, D.C.: The Alban Institute (March-April 1991).

Pappas, Anthony G. *Entering the World of the Small Church: A Guide for Church Leaders.* Washington, DC: The Alban Institute, 1988.

———. *Money, Motivation, and Mission in the Small Church.* Small Church in Action Series. Edited by Douglas Alan Walrath. Valley Forge, Pa.: Judson Press, 1989.

———. *Mustard Seeds: Devotions for Small Church People.* Columbus, Ga.: Brentwood Christian Press, 1994.

———, and Scott Planting. *Mission: The Small Church Reaches Out.* Small Church in Action Series. Edited by Douglas Alan Walrath. Valley Forge, Pa.: Judson Press, 1993.

Planting, Scott. "Local Mission in the Small Church." *The Five Stones* (Spring 1991).

Poage, Bennet, ed. *The Tobacco Church: A Manual for Congregational Leaders.* Richmond, Va.: Kentucky Appalachia Ministry, 1993.

Ray, David R. *Small Churches Are the Right Size.* New York: Pilgrim Press, 1982.

———. *The Big Small Church Book.* Cleveland, Ohio: Pilgrim Press, 1992.

Robinson, Martin, and Dan Yarnell. *Celebrating the Small Church.* Tunbridge Wells, Kent, England: Monarch, 1993.

Roper, Hazel A. "Two Cultures Experience People Helping People," *The American Baptist* (November-December 1986).

Rothauge, Arlin J. *Sizing Up a Congregation for New Member Ministry.* New York: The Education for Mission and Ministry Office, The Episcopal Church Center, n.d..

Rowthorn, Anne. *The Liberation of the Laity.* Wilton, Conn.: Morehouse-Barlow, 1986.

Saarinen, Martin F. *The Life Cycle of a Congregation.* Washington, D.C.: The Alban Institute, 1990.

Schaller, Lyle E. *The Pastor and the People.* Nashville: Abingdon Press, 1973.

————. *The Small Church Is Different!* Nashville: Abingdon Press, 1982.

————. *Looking in the Mirror: Self-Appraisal in the Local Church.* Nashville: Abingdon Press, 1984.

————. *The Small Membership Church: Scenarios for Tomorrow.* Nashville: Abingdon Press, 1994.

Schirer, Marshal E. and Mary Anne Forehand. *Cooperative Ministry: Hope for Small Churches.* Valley Forge, Pa.: Judson Press, 1984.

Schuller, Robert H. *Self-Esteem: The New Reformation.* Waco, Tex.: Word, 1982.

Sim, R. Alex. *The Plight of the Rural Church.* Toronto, Canada: The United Church Publishing House, 1990.

Sims, Rose. *New Life for Dying Churches! It Can Happen Anywhere.* Trilby, Fla.: New Life Church Growth Ministries, 1994.

Smith, Norris. "Forced Termination: Scope and Response." *Search.* 21, no. 1 (Fall 1990).

Steinke, Peter L. *How Your Church Family Works: Understanding Congregations as Emotional Systems.* Washington, D.C.: Alban Institute, 1993.

————. *Healthy Congregations: A Systems Approach.* Washington, D.C.: Alban Institute, 1996.

Strawn, Elaine, and Christine Nees. *Fifteen Services for Small Churches.* Nashville: Abingdon Press, 1993.

Surrey, Peter. *The Small Town Church.* Creative Leadership Series. Edited by Lyle E. Schaller. Nashville: Abingdon Press, 1981.

Wagley, Laurence A. *Preaching with the Small Congregation.* Nashville: Abingdon Press, 1989.

Waldkoenig, Gilson A.C., and William O. Avery. *Cooperating Congregations: Portraits of Mission Strategies.* Washington, D.C.: The Alban Institute, 2000.

Walrath, Douglas Alan. *Leading Churches Through Change.* Creative Leadership Series. Edited by Lyle E. Schaller. Nashville: Abingdon Press, 1979.

———. *Finding Options for Ministry in Small Churches: A Report to the Program Committee for Professional Church Leadership.* New York: National Council of Churches, 1981.

———. *Planning for Your Church.* Philadelphia: Westminster Press, 1984.

———. *Options: How to Develop and Share Christian Faith Today.* New York: Pilgrim Press, 1988.

———. *Frameworks: Patterns for Living and Believing Today.* New York: Pilgrim Press, 1991.

———. *Making It Work: Effective Administration in the Small Church.* Small Church in Action Series. Edited by Douglas Alan Walrath. Valley Forge, Pa.: Judson Press, 1994.

———, ed. *New Possibilities for Small Churches.* New York: Pilgrim Press, 1983.

———, and Sherry Walrath. *Church and Ministry in Rural Culture Today.* Bangor, Maine: Bangor Theological Seminary.

Whiteside, Lee. "Healing the Dreaded Census Preventsus." *The Small Church Newsletter* (September 1991).

Willimon, William H., and Robert L. Wilson. *Preaching and Worship in the Small Church.* Nashville: Abingdon, 1980.

Zunkel, Wayne. *Growing the Small Church: A Guide for Church Leaders.* Elgin, Ill.: David C. Cook Publishing Co., 1982.

Periodicals

The Five Stones (quarterly journal). Edited by Anthony G. Pappas, 69
  Weymouth, Providence, Rhode Island 02906.

The Small Church Newsletter (quarterly publication). Edited by John
  Bennett, MSR Center for Rural Ministry, PO Box 104685,
  Jefferson City, Missouri 65110-4685.

The United Methodist Rural Fellowship Bulletin (quarterly
  publication). Edited by Mel West, 108 Balow Wynd, Columbia,
  Missouri 65203.

PEDRO GOES BUGGY

by Fran Manushkin

illustrated by
Tammie Lyon

PICTURE WINDOW BOOKS
a capstone imprint

Pedro is published by Picture Window Books,
a Capstone Imprint
1710 Roe Crest Drive
North Mankato, Minnesota 56003
www.mycapstone.com

Library of Congress Cataloging-in-Publication Data
Names: Manushkin, Fran, author. | Lyon, Tammie, illustrator.
Title: Pedro goes buggy / by Fran Manushkin ; [illustrator, Tammie Lyon].
Description: North Mankato, Minnesota : Picture Window Books, an imprint of Capstone Press, [2017] | Series: Pedro | Summary: Pedro collects a lot of different bugs for a class assignment, but when his brother lets them out in the house their parents are furious, and ban any further collecting.
Identifiers: LCCN 2015046881| ISBN 9781515800859 (library binding) | ISBN 9781515800897 (pbk.) | ISBN 9781515800934 (ebook (pdf))
Subjects: LCSH: Hispanic Americans—Juvenile fiction. | Brothers—Juvenile fiction. | Insects—Juvenile fiction. | Science projects—Juvenile fiction. | CYAC: Hispanic Americans—Fiction. | Brothers—Fiction. | Insects—Fiction. | Science projects—Fiction.
Classification: LCC PZ7.M3195 Pc 2017 | DDC 813.54—dc23
LC record available at http://lccn.loc.gov/2015046881

Designer: Aruna Rangarajan and Tracy McCabe

Design Elements: Shutterstock

Photo Credits:
Greg Holch, pg. 26
Tammie Lyon, pg. 26

Printed and bound in the USA.
001725

Table of Contents

Chapter 1
Wild About Bugs

"Who likes bugs?" asked

Miss Winkle.

"I do!" yelled Pedro. "I am

wild about bugs!"

"Me too," said Katie Woo. "I like the green bugs that are called katydids."

"Ha!" Pedro smiled. "You would!"

"We are going to study bugs," said Miss Winkle. "After school, go out and look for bugs. Pick one that you like and write about it."

"I like stinkbugs!" shouted

Roddy. "I can bring one to

school. That would be fun!"

"Not a good

idea," said

Miss Winkle.

Pedro went home and

found his bug jar.

He began looking for bugs

in the weeds. He found ten

ants and put them in his jar.

Pedro told JoJo, "Flies are fun too. But they are hard to catch."

"Not for my cat," bragged JoJo.

"Spiders are cool," Pedro told his mother. "I'll bring some home."

"No way!" said his mom. "Ants are fine, but no spiders!"

Pedro found a field with
lots of ladybugs. He took
home fifteen. His puppy,
Peppy, tried to eat them.

"No way!" yelled Pedro.

Pedro loved

beetles too.

"They are so

shiny," he told JoJo.

"And they are fun to say," he

added. "Beetle, beetle, beetle!"

He took home twenty.

Chapter 2
Bed Bugs, Head Bugs

Pedro couldn't stop

catching bugs! Each day he

found more.

He told his little brother,

Paco, "It's a good thing I have

a big jar!"

One day, when Pedro was at school, Paco told the bugs, "I want to watch you run around."

He opened the jar and let them out!

There were bugs on the bed

and bugs on Paco's head.

"Cool!" he said.

When Pedro came home,

he said, "Not cool!"

"Out they go!" said Pedro's dad. "These bugs are driving me buggy."

Chapter 3
Get Hopping

The next day, Pedro told Katie, "I have no bugs to write about."

"You better hurry and find one," said Katie. "Get hopping."

"I love hopping!" said Pedro. He hopped down the block looking for a new bug.

He saw a wasp. "No way!" he yelled.

He saw a grasshopper

jumping in the weeds.

"Let's race!" Pedro yelled.

Pedro hopped. Then the grasshopper jumped.

"It's a tie!" yelled JoJo. "You both win!"

Pedro told the grasshopper, "You are the most fun. I will write about you."

Pedro wrote about the grasshopper. Then he let him go.

"Good work," said Miss Winkle. "Next we will be writing about tigers."

"Great!" Pedro smiled. "I can't wait to bring one home."

About the Author

Fran Manushkin is the author of many popular picture books, including *Happy in Our Skin*; *Baby, Come Out!*; *Latkes and Applesauce: A Hanukkah Story*; *The Tushy Book*; *The Belly Book*; and *Big Girl Panties*. Fran writes on her beloved Mac computer in New York City, without the help of her two naughty cats, Chaim and Goldy.

About the Illustrator

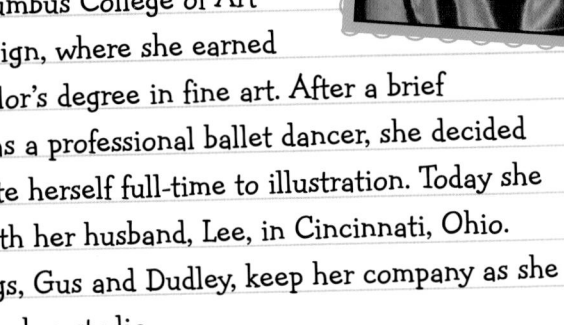

Tammie Lyon began her love for drawing at a young age while sitting at the kitchen table with her dad. She continued her love of art and eventually attended the Columbus College of Art and Design, where she earned a bachelor's degree in fine art. After a brief career as a professional ballet dancer, she decided to devote herself full-time to illustration. Today she lives with her husband, Lee, in Cincinnati, Ohio. Her dogs, Gus and Dudley, keep her company as she works in her studio.

Glossary

bragged (BRAGD)—talked about how good you are at something

katydid (KAY-tee-did)—a large, green bug that is like a grasshopper

shiny (SHY-nee)—very smooth and bright

wasp (WOSP)—a flying bug that has a thin body; female wasps can give a painful sting

wild (WILDE)—going beyond what is usual

Let's Talk

1. Pedro loves all kinds of bugs. What's your favorite type of bug? Why do you like it?

2. Miss Winkle tells the kids to go out and look for bugs to write about. Where does Pedro find bugs? Where would you go to look for bugs?

3. Pedro's mom does not like spiders. How do we know that? Which bugs don't you like?

Let's Write

1. Pedro writes about a grasshopper. Write down three facts about your favorite bug. If you can't think of three, ask a grown-up to help you find some in a book or on the computer.

2. Draw a picture of what your favorite bug looks like. Then write a short story about it.

3. Think about all the different types of bugs that Pedro caught in his jar. Write them down in a list. Then write the names of all the other types of bugs you can think of.

JOKE AROUND

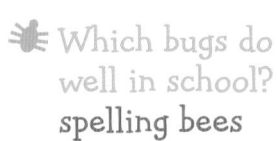

🐜 Which bugs do
well in school?
spelling bees

🐜 Name the fastest bug in the world.
the quicket

🐜 Which insects are knows for their
good manners?
ladybugs

🐜 What is the biggest ant in the world?
an elephant

🐜 What do spiders like with their
hamburgers?
French flies

Soil

by Chris Bowman

BELLWETHER MEDIA · MINNEAPOLIS, MN

Note to Librarians, Teachers, and Parents:

Blastoff! Readers are carefully developed by literacy experts and combine standards-based content with developmentally appropriate text.

Level 1 provides the most support through repetition of high-frequency words, light text, predictable sentence patterns, and strong visual support.

Level 2 offers early readers a bit more challenge through varied simple sentences, increased text load, and less repetition of high-frequency words.

Level 3 advances early-fluent readers toward fluency through increased text and concept load, less reliance on visuals, longer sentences, and more literary language.

Level 4 builds reading stamina by providing more text per page, increased use of punctuation, greater variation in sentence patterns, and increasingly challenging vocabulary.

Level 5 encourages children to move from "learning to read" to "reading to learn" by providing even more text, varied writing styles, and less familiar topics.

Whichever book is right for your reader, Blastoff! Readers are the perfect books to build confidence and encourage a love of reading that will last a lifetime!

This edition first published in 2016 by Bellwether Media, Inc.

No part of this publication may be reproduced in whole or in part without written permission of the publisher. For information regarding permission, write to Bellwether Media, Inc., Attention: Permissions Department, 6012 Blue Circle Dr., Minnetonka, MN 55343.

Library of Congress Cataloging-in-Publication Data
Bowman, Chris, 1990- author.
  Soil / by Chris Bowman.
     pages cm. – (Blastoff! Readers. Earth Science Rocks!)
  Summary: "Developed by literacy experts for students in kindergarten through grade three, this book introduces soil to young readers through leveled text and related photos"– Provided by publisher.
  Audience: Ages 5-8.
  Audience: K to grade 3.
  Includes bibliographical references and index.
  ISBN: 978-1-60014-982-5 (hardcover : alk. paper)
  ISBN: 978-1-62617-498-6 (paperback : alk. paper)
  1. Soils–Juvenile literature. 2. Soil formation–Juvenile literature. I. Title.
  S591.3.B636 2014
  551.3'05–dc23
                    2014008247

Table of Contents

What Is Soil?

Soil is the top layer of the earth. It is a mix of **minerals** and pieces of rock.

4

The **remains** of plants and animals are in it, too. Soil also holds air and water.

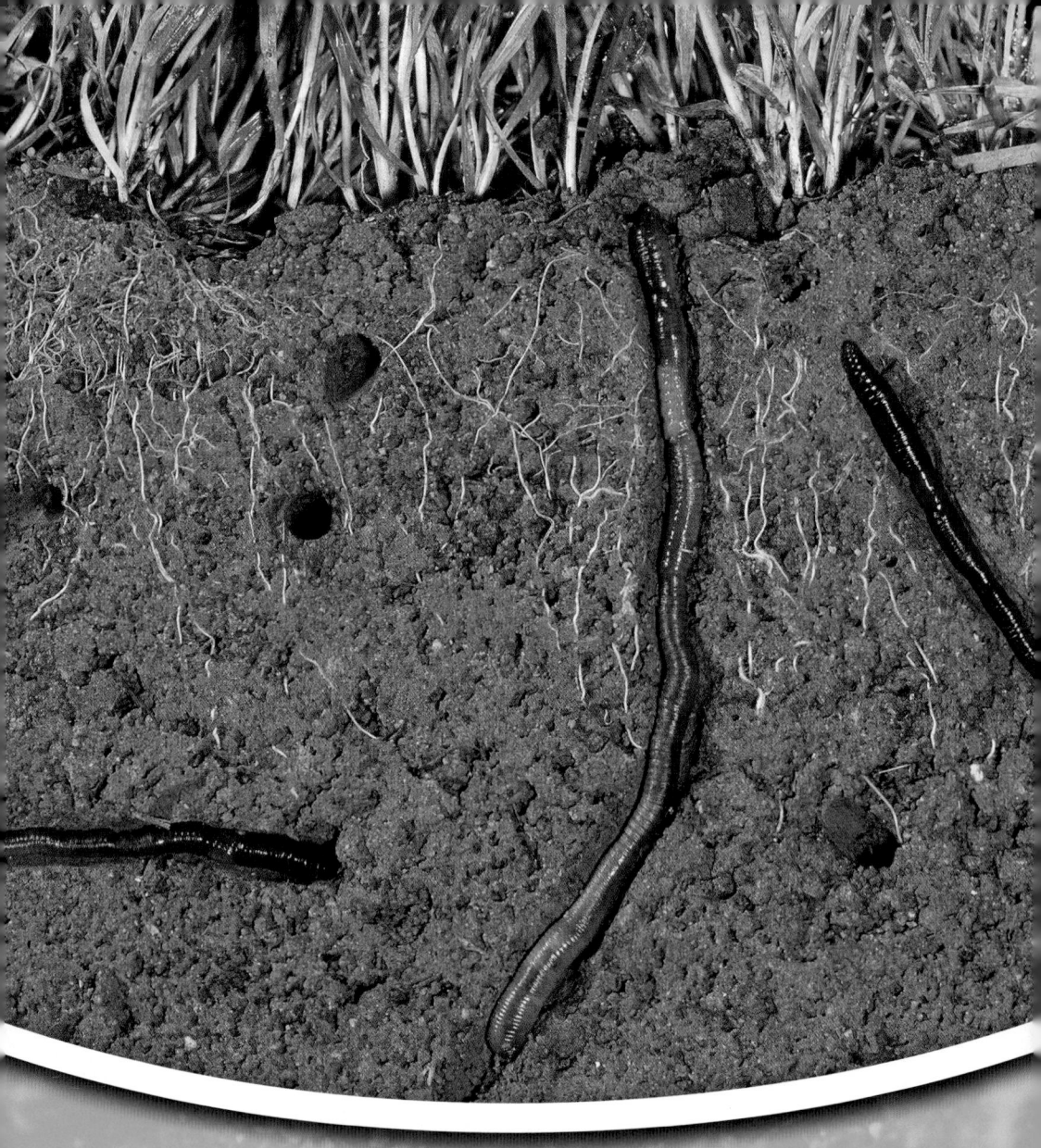

Earthworms, mice, and other animals dig **burrows** in soil. Plant roots grow in it.

Earth's Layers

Earth is made up of the inner core, outer core, mantle, and crust. Soils are found on the top of the crust.

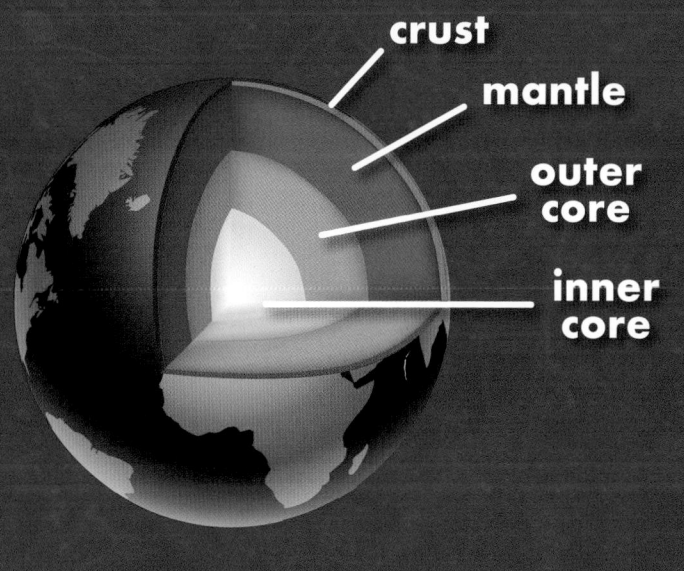

crust

mantle

outer core

inner core

Soil stores and cleans water. It also filters **pollution** from the air.

How Soil Forms

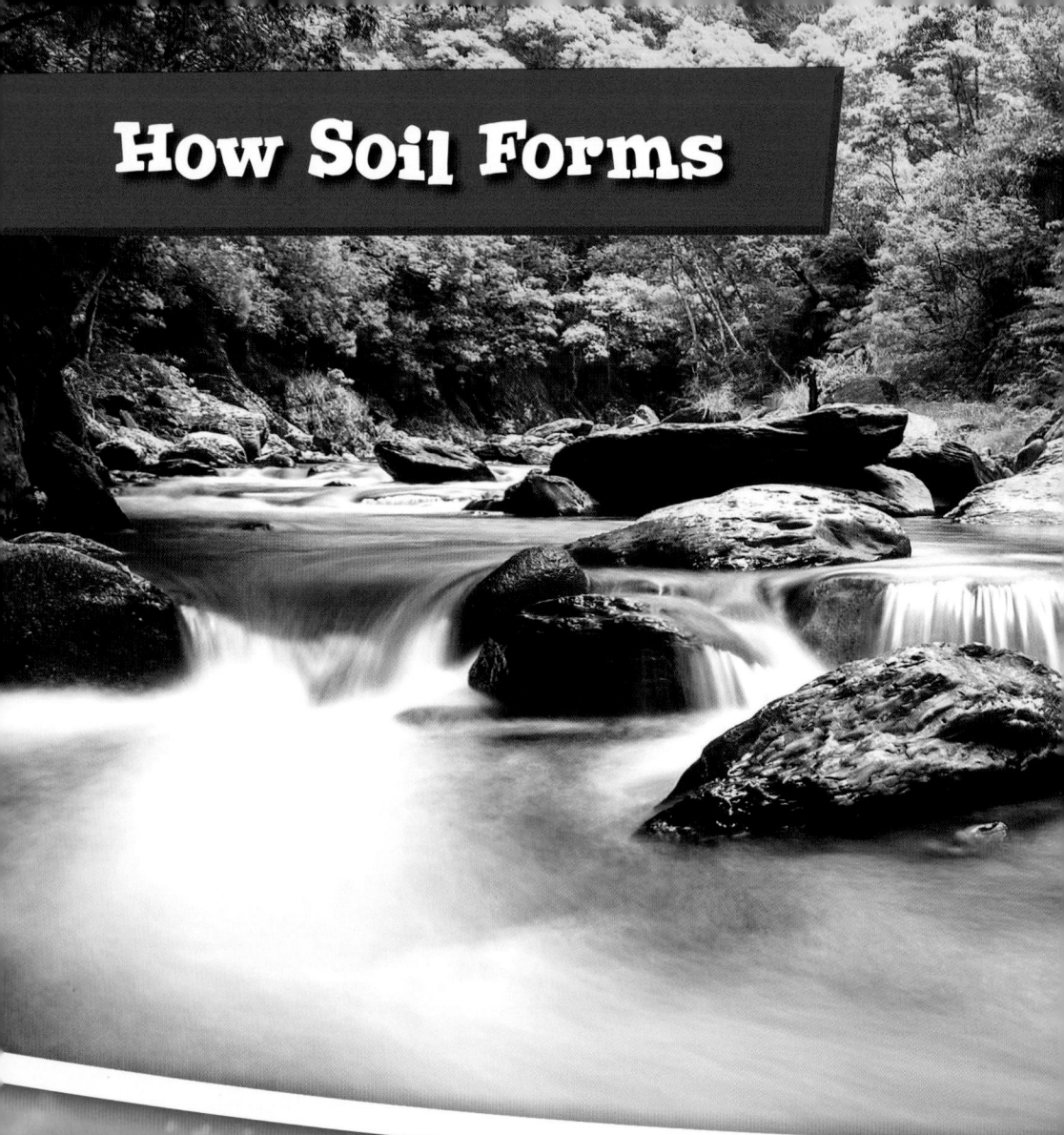

Many processes work together to form soil. **Weathering** breaks big rocks into smaller pieces.

Erosion wears down and moves
the pieces.

Tiny **microbes** help break down dead plants and animals. The plants and animals **decay**. They become **humus**. This is thick and dark in color.

humus

Soil Horizons

The soil in the ground is often made up of layers called soil horizons. Each layer is a different type of soil.

O horizon
(top layer)

A horizon
(surface soil)

B horizon
(subsoil)

C horizon
(parent rock)

R horizon
(bedrock)

Types of Soil

There are six main types of soil. Clay clumps and feels slimy when wet. It gets hard when it dries out.

clay

silt

Silt holds a lot of water and air. It has a smooth feel.

chalky soil

Chalky soil is full of rocks. Plants do not grow well here.

Sand covers beaches and deserts. It is a **gritty** soil.

sand

Peat is dark in color. It contains a lot of humus and water. **Loam** is sometimes called the perfect soil. It is full of **nutrients**. Gardens and farms often have this soil.

loam

peat

Soil as a Clue

Pedologists are scientists who study soil. They take soil samples to learn about an environment. A soil sample can tell about the air quality and rainfall in an area.

Digging in Soil

Soil covers the ground all around us. More than 70,000 kinds have been identified in the United States. Get your hands dirty and discover many kinds!

Be a Pedologist!

What you need:

glass jar	soil	water

1. Fill the jar about 1/3 full of soil.

2. Fill the rest of the jar with water. Put the lid on tightly.

3. Shake the jar until the contents are mixed well.

4. Let it sit for two days.

5. Look at the jar. Can you see layers? These are different types of soil!

Glossary

burrows—holes in the ground that some animals dig

decay—to rot or break down

erosion—the process of wearing away

gritty—being made of small pieces

humus—plant and animal remains after being broken down; humus is a part of soil.

loam—soil that supports plant growth

microbes—living things that are too small to see with the naked eye

minerals—solid substances found in nature

nutrients—substances that provide energy for plants and animals to grow

peat—a type of soil that holds a lot of water; peat is often found in swamps and bogs.

pedologists—scientists who study soils

pollution—a harmful substance damaging an environment

remains—the bodies of dead plants and animals

silt—a type of soil made of small grains

weathering—the process of breaking rocks into smaller pieces

To Learn More

AT THE LIBRARY

Aloian, Molly. *Different Kinds of Soil*. New York, N.Y.: Crabtree Pub. Co., 2009.

Hyde, Natalie. *Micro Life in Soil*. New York, N.Y.: Crabtree Pub. Co., 2010.

Petersen, Christine. *Super Soils*. Edina, Minn.: ABDO Pub., 2010.

ON THE WEB

Learning more about soil is as easy as 1, 2, 3.

1. Go to www.factsurfer.com.

2. Enter "soil" into the search box.

3. Click the "Surf" button and you will see a list of related web sites.

With factsurfer.com, finding more information is just a click away.

Index

The images in this book are reproduced through the courtesy of: romrf, front cover; Igor Stramyk, pp. 4-5; Jean-Paul Ferrero/ Age Fotostock, p. 6; Webspark, p. 7; NH, pp. 8-9; Monchai Tudsamalee, p. 10; Jon Eppard, p. 11; tartaro/ Canstock, p. 12; alexmak72427, p. 13; Biosphoto/ SuperStock, p. 14; burkovsky, p. 15; Sheila Terry/ Science Source, p. 16; Photos Lamontagne/ Getty Images, p. 17; Ted Wood/ Aurora Photos/ Corbis, p. 18; Citira Limited/ SuperStock, p. 19; Steve Debenport, p. 20; Graham Taylor Photography, p. 21 (left); Tischenko Irina, p. 21 (middle); design56, p. 21 (right).